COMPACT *Research*

Mood
Disorders

Diseases and Disorders

ReferencePoint
Press®

San Diego, CA

Select* books in the Compact Research series include:

Current Issues

Abortion
Animal Experimentation
Conflict in the Middle East
The Death Penalty
DNA Evidence and
    Investigation
Drugs and Sports
Energy Alternatives
Gangs
Genetic Testing
Global Warming and
    Climate Change

Gun Control
Islam
National Security
Nuclear Weapons and
    Security
Obesity
Online Social Networking
Stem Cells
Teen Smoking
Terrorist Attacks
Video Games
World Energy Crisis

Diseases and Disorders

ADHD
Anorexia
Bipolar Disorders
Drug Addiction
HPV
Influenza

Obsessive-Compulsive
    Disorder
Phobias
Post-Traumatic Stress
    Disorder
Sexually Transmitted
    Diseases

Drugs

Antidepressants
Club Drugs
Cocaine and Crack
Hallucinogens
Heroin
Inhalants
Marijuana

Methamphetamine
Nicotine and Tobacco
Painkillers
Performance-Enhancing
    Drugs
Prescription Drugs
Steroids

Energy and the Environment

Coal Power
Deforestation
Garbage and Recycling

Solar Power
Toxic Waste
Wind Power

*For a complete list of titles please visit www.referencepointpress.com.

Mood Disorders

Carla Mooney

Diseases and Disorders

ReferencePoint
Press®

San Diego, CA

© 2011 ReferencePoint Press, Inc.

For more information, contact:
ReferencePoint Press, Inc.
PO Box 27779
San Diego, CA 92198
www. ReferencePointPress.com

LIBRARY OF CONGRESS CATALOGING-IN-PUBLICATION DATA

Mooney, Carla, 1970–
  Mood disorders / by Carla Mooney.
    p. cm. — (Compact research)
  Includes bibliographical references and index.
  ISBN-13: 978-1-60152-119-4 (hardback)
  ISBN-10: 1-60152-119-7 (hardback)
  1. Affective disorders—Popular works. I. Title.
  RC537.M6647   2010
  616.85'27—dc22
                                        2010005868

Contents

Foreword

66Where is the knowledge we have lost in information?99

—T.S. Eliot, "The Rock."

As modern civilization continues to evolve, its ability to create, store, distribute, and access information expands exponentially. The explosion of information from all media continues to increase at a phenomenal rate. By 2020 some experts predict the worldwide information base will double every 73 days. While access to diverse sources of information and perspectives is paramount to any democratic society, information alone cannot help people gain knowledge and understanding. Information must be organized and presented clearly and succinctly in order to be understood. The challenge in the digital age becomes not the creation of information, but how best to sort, organize, enhance, and present information.

ReferencePoint Press developed the *Compact Research* series with this challenge of the information age in mind. More than any other subject area today, researching current issues can yield vast, diverse, and unqualified information that can be intimidating and overwhelming for even the most advanced and motivated researcher. The *Compact Research* series offers a compact, relevant, intelligent, and conveniently organized collection of information covering a variety of current topics ranging from illegal immigration and deforestation to diseases such as anorexia and meningitis.

The series focuses on three types of information: objective single-author narratives, opinion-based primary source quotations, and facts and statistics. The clearly written objective narratives provide context and reliable background information. Primary source quotes are carefully selected and cited, exposing the reader to differing points of view. And facts and statistics sections aid the reader in evaluating perspectives. Presenting these key types of information creates a richer, more balanced learning experience.

For better understanding and convenience, the series enhances information by organizing it into narrower topics and adding design features that make it easy for a reader to identify desired content. For example, in *Compact Research: Illegal Immigration*, a chapter covering the economic impact of illegal immigration has an objective narrative explaining the various ways the economy is impacted, a balanced section of numerous primary source quotes on the topic, followed by facts and full-color illustrations to encourage evaluation of contrasting perspectives.

The ancient Roman philosopher Lucius Annaeus Seneca wrote, "It is quality rather than quantity that matters." More than just a collection of content, the *Compact Research* series is simply committed to creating, finding, organizing, and presenting the most relevant and appropriate amount of information on a current topic in a user-friendly style that invites, intrigues, and fosters understanding.

Mood Disorders at a Glance

Mood Disorders Defined

Mood disorders are mental illnesses that affect the way people think and feel about themselves and the world around them. If untreated, a mood disorder can interfere with a person's daily life and ability to function.

Two Main Categories of Mood Disorders

There are two main categories of mood disorders—unipolar and bipolar. Unipolar disorders cause people to have a depressed mood. Bipolar mood disorders cause severe mood swings.

Prevalence of Mood Disorders

According to the National Institute of Mental Health, each year approximately 10 percent of people in the United States over the age of 18 have a mood disorder.

Signs and Symptoms

Symptoms of a depressive mood disorder include persistent sadness, changes in sleep patterns and appetite, fatigue, and feelings of worthlessness and self-hate. Symptoms of the manic phase of bipolar disorder include intense euphoria or irritability.

Causes

Most experts believe that mood disorders are caused by a combination of genetic, biological, and environmental factors.

Effects of Mood Disorders

Mood disorders often impair a person's ability to sleep, eat, and work, as well as damage a person's relationships with family and friends. Mood disorders can also lead to poor decisions and risky behavior.

Treatment

Most people treated for mood disorders see an improvement in their symptoms within four to six weeks. Medication, counseling, electroconvulsive therapy, and lifestyle changes have all been effective in managing mood disorder symptoms.

Prognosis

Mood disorders are often lifelong conditions. Effective treatments can help manage symptoms so that people with mood disorders can lead normal, productive lives.

Overview

"Most times, I feel my future has no promise. . . . Every time I think my future is hopeful, something comes along and destroys the hope . . . it was all because I suffer from depression; the disease you can't see or touch, and that many think is all 'in your head.'"

—Debbie, a major depression and dysthymia patient.

What Are Mood Disorders?

E veryone feels blue or sad at times. For most people these feelings pass within a couple of days. For others they linger and become something more serious. Mood disorders are a group of mental illnesses that affect the way people think and feel about the world around them. They interfere with a person's daily life and ability to function. Although there are several types of mood disorders, most include periods of depression. The depression may vary in length and intensity. For people with bipolar disorder, which is one type of mood disorder, depression may also be accompanied by periods of mania. When in a manic state, a person experiences an abnormally elevated or irritated mood.

Mood disorders are some of the oldest illnesses in the history of medicine. In the fourth century B.C., doctors believed that a mood disorder—or "melancholia," as they called it—was a physical illness caused by an excess of black bile in the body. By the nineteenth century doctors redefined melancholia. They viewed it as a psychological disorder. Today experts know that mood disorders have a combination of physical and psychological symptoms.

There are two main categories of mood disorders—unipolar and bipolar. People with unipolar disorders feel sad and have depressive symptoms. Major depression, dysthymia, seasonal affective disorder (SAD), and postpartum depression are all types of unipolar disorders.

Bipolar mood disorders cause severe mood swings. During a down phase, people with bipolar disorder can become deeply depressed. Other times they swing high into a mania and seem extremely elated or active. For this reason bipolar disorder is also known as manic depression.

According to the National Institute of Mental Health, in a given year approximately 9.5 percent of people in the United States over the age of 18 have a mood disorder. Major depression is the most common mood disorder, with almost 7 percent of the U.S. population over the age of 18 affected by it. Approximately 2.6 percent of American adults over age 18 are affected by bipolar disorder in a given year.

In the United States women are twice as likely as men are to be diagnosed and treated for major depression. As children, boys and girls have equal rates of depression. When girls reach adolescence, however, they are more likely to become depressed. This increased risk follows them into adulthood. Unlike depression, bipolar disorder generally occurs in men and women equally.

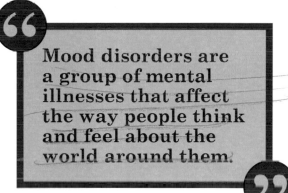

" Mood disorders are a group of mental illnesses that affect the way people think and feel about the world around them. "

If a person has had depression or bipolar disorder before, his or her chances of developing it again increase. Approximately 50 percent of people who have experienced a depressive episode will have future episodes. For people with bipolar disorder, the risk is even higher. Most affected people will experience repeated episodes of mania. Because they are likely to recur, most mood disorders are considered long-term or chronic illnesses.

In 2004 Terrie Williams owned a successful public relations agency. On the outside Terrie was the ultimate professional, juggling her clients and workload with ease. On the inside, however, she felt out of control. "As my agency grew, I became so overwhelmed by the length of my to-do list that I could barely get out of bed. . . . I didn't recognize what was going on with me. . . . Some mornings, I'd be on the floor in tears and an hour later, I'd be at work,"[1] she says. Eventually, close friends encouraged Terrie to see a therapist, who diagnosed her with clinical depression. "I felt such relief to know that something was actually wrong with me, that it wasn't all in my head. There was a name for it and it could be fixed. For the first time in a long time, I had hope,"[2] she says.

Many Different Symptoms

No two people experience mood disorders in the same way. While everyone is sad at times, if the sadness is very intense or lasts more than two weeks, it may be a sign of a mood disorder. Those with depressive disorders generally experience a severe sadness that interferes with their life. They may lose interest in activities they once enjoyed and withdraw from family and friends. Feelings of hopelessness and worthlessness are also common. Depressive disorders cause physical symptoms like headaches, stomachaches, and fatigue. Sleeping and eating patterns may also change.

Courtney remembers how she felt during a depressive episode. "I was sixteen and sitting in my room, crying uncontrollably. I tried to think what was making me so sad, but I didn't know. I just didn't feel right, but I didn't know why I was so sad. That's the worst part about it—crying and feeling like your world is ending but not knowing what is causing you to ache."[3]

With bipolar disorder, manic periods alternate with depressive phases. During a manic phase, a person may be intensely euphoric. Others might be extremely irritable. They might talk fast and seem to be moving at hyperspeed. They might feel invincible, take risks, and show poor judgment. The manic and depressive periods can vary in duration and intensity. Missy, a 42-year-old with bipolar disorder, says that during a manic phase, "I had very high energy and stopped sleeping. I went from eight hours of sleep a night down to three hours of sleep. I wasn't even tired. My thoughts were racing, and I was going a million miles an hour. One night, I didn't sleep at all."[4]

What Causes Mood Disorders?

The causes of mood disorders are not well understood. Mental health experts believe that there is no single cause. Instead, they suspect that a combination of biological, environmental, and genetic factors play a part in mood disorders. The causes of mood disorders are different for every person. Sometimes people become depressed even when everything in their life is going right. Other people develop a mood disorder in reaction to stressful or traumatic events. Because each person reacts differently to these factors, it is often difficult to predict who will develop a mood disorder.

Mental health experts believe that chemical imbalances in the brain are connected to mood disorders. Chemicals called neurotransmitters affect how a person thinks, feels, and acts. Neurotransmitters carry messages from the brain to different parts of the body. In people with mood disorders, these chemicals can get out of balance and the messages can be lost or distorted, leading to depressive symptoms. Scientists have also found that the brain cells of bipolar patients often have a buildup of calcium. While calcium is an important mineral for strong bones and teeth, too much of the mineral in brain cells has been found to affect neurological function.

Depressive disorders cause physical symptoms like headaches, stomachaches, and fatigue.

Hormone imbalances may be another factor in mood disorders. Researchers know that some hormones directly affect the brain chemistry that controls emotions and mood. They have found that many people with mood disorders have abnormal levels of certain hormones in their blood. For example, cortisol is a hormone that helps the body regulate its reaction to stress. About 50 percent of people with clinical depression have an excess of cortisol in their blood.

Environmental factors can also increase the risk of developing a mood disorder. For many people a stressful event like the death of a loved one, a job loss, or the end of a relationship triggers a depressive episode. Not everyone experiencing stress, however, develops a mood disorder. The exact same event may lead to a mood disorder for one person, but not another. Other environmental factors that can influence mood disorders include traumatic events, injuries, and abuse. In addition, how a person copes with stress and the availability of a support network may influence whether or not he or she develops a mood disorder.

Genetic Risk Factors

People of all ages, races, and social status develop mood disorders. No one is immune to these illnesses. Certain groups of people, however, tend to experience mood disorders more often than others. Research has shown that people from families with a history of mood disorders have a greater risk of developing a mood disorder themselves. A person with a parent or sibling with major depression is one and a half to three times more likely to develop the disorder than a person with no such family history.

Bipolar disease has an even stronger family connection. Fifty percent of people with bipolar disorder have a parent with a history of clinical depression. A child with one parent with bipolar disorder has a 25 percent greater chance of developing the disorder. If both parents have it, the child's risk increases to between 50 and 75 percent. These findings suggest that there is a genetic link to mood disorders. However, scientists are still figuring out which genes are involved and how they influence mood disorders. "Mental disorders are the most complex of all diseases," says researcher Kathleen Ries Merikangas of the National Institute of Mental Health's Mood and Anxiety Disorders Program. "We're learning more about how genes can control the different biologic pathways in the brain, but more importantly, how that brain is wired to respond to environmental factors. We're at the very primitive stages of knowledge."[5]

> **Mental health experts believe that chemical imbalances in the brain are connected to mood disorders.**

How Do Mood Disorders Affect People?

Mood disorders can affect a person's life in many ways. Physically, they interfere with sleeping and eating patterns. Mood disorders can cause physical illnesses like headaches, stomachaches, back pain, and fatigue. These changes affect how people perform at work or at school. They may have difficulty concentrating or miss days because of their illness. According to the World Health Organization, major depression is the leading cause of disability in the United States for people ages 15 to 44. It is one of the top workplace issues and costs U.S. businesses about $70 billion each year in medical expenses, worker absences, and lost productivity.

Brenda remembers the impact depression had on her daily life:

> It was really hard to get out of bed in the morning. I just wanted to hide under the covers and not talk to anyone. I didn't feel much like eating and I lost a lot of weight. Nothing seemed fun anymore. I was tired all the time, yet I wasn't sleeping well at night. But I knew that I had to keep going because I've got kids and a job. It just felt so impossible, like nothing was going to change or get better. I started missing days from work, and a friend noticed that something wasn't right.[6]

Many people with mood disorders begin to act differently around family and friends. They may withdraw and prefer to be alone. Activities that once interested them may no longer seem appealing. Insignificant events might trigger crying episodes or anger and fights. This erratic behavior can affect relationships. Family and friends may have a difficult time understanding why a person's behavior has changed.

Mood disorders also have a dramatic emotional impact. People can experience extreme emotions for no apparent reason. In addition, having a mood disorder can damage a person's self-esteem and confidence. During a depressive episode, Rob found he had trouble controlling his emotions, which affected how he acted around his family. "At first I was feeling sad all the time, even though I had no reason to be. Then the sadness turned into anger, and I started having fights with my family and friends. I felt really bad about myself, like I wasn't good enough for anyone. It got so bad that I wished I would go to bed and never wake,"[7] he says.

Risky Behavior

People with mood disorders are more likely to abuse alcohol, drugs, or tobacco. Many find they cannot cope with their feelings of sadness and depression. As a result, they turn to alcohol, drugs, or tobacco to change how they feel. People with bipolar disorder in a manic phase may use drugs and alcohol to enhance their high. A study published in January 2008 showed that people with mood disorders, particularly mania and bipolar disorder, had a higher risk of developing a substance abuse problem.

People with mood disorders are more likely to abuse alcohol and drugs. Many find that they cannot cope with their feelings of sadness and depression and turn to alcohol and drugs for relief.

"The findings confirm the link between mood disorders and substance abuse or dependence problems," said Merikangas. "They also suggest that earlier detection of bipolar symptoms could help to prevent subsequent substance abuse problems."[8]

Using drugs and alcohol to numb feelings may work in the short term, but substance abuse makes a person feel worse over time. "At the time it felt good to be more popular, and I was happy when I was drunk," says Darren, who turned to alcohol to cope with his depression. "But deep down I knew it was all superficial."[9] Mood disorders have also been connected to other risky behaviors like self-cutting, unprotected and promiscuous sexual activity, and eating disorders.

High Risk of Suicide

Untreated mood disorders can increase the risk of suicide. According to the Centers for Disease Control and Prevention, more than 33,000 people in the United States kill themselves each year. In 2006, the most recent year for which data are available, suicide was the eleventh leading cause of death for all ages. More than 90 percent of those who committed suicide had a mental disorder, most commonly a depressive or substance abuse disorder. For teens and young adults, depression is the number one risk factor for suicide.

Sixteen-year-old Jayme admits to spending hours thinking about death and her funeral when she was depressed. "I'd think about who would come; what people would say about me and if anyone would miss me if I died. I also thought a lot about different ways I could take my

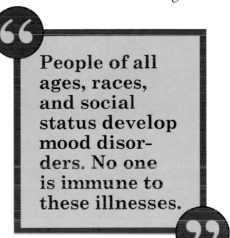

People of all ages, races, and social status develop mood disorders. No one is immune to these illnesses.

life and which would be the most painless," she says. "I remember sitting at a busy intersection at a stop light, and I very seriously thought about what would happen if I were to just take my foot off the brake."[10]

Diagnosing Mood Disorders

If depressive symptoms are severe and last for two weeks or more, it may be time to seek help. Untreated mood disorders can linger for weeks, months, or years. As time passes they often grow worse and become more difficult to treat.

A doctor or mental health expert can diagnose a patient with a mood disorder. At the first appointment the mental health expert will usually ask the patient questions in order to evaluate his or her condition. Special questionnaires called mental health inventories record a patient's feelings, physical symptoms, and daily experiences and can help with diagnosis. During the evaluation the mental health professional will also look for any medications, illnesses, or physical conditions that may be causing depressive symptoms. Some types of strokes, thyroid disorders, and contraceptives can cause the same symptoms as a mood disorder. If the mental health professional determines that the patient has a mood disorder, he or she will work with the patient to develop an appropriate treatment plan.

What Treatments Are Available for Mood Disorders?

Although mood disorders are serious illnesses, they can be treated. With psychotherapy, medication, or a combination treatment, most people can manage their mood disorder and lead a productive life. According to the National Institutes of Health, up to 80 percent of people treated for depressive mood disorders show improvement within four to six weeks.

Most treatments for mood disorders involve some type of psychotherapy, also known as talk therapy. Talk therapy can be individual, group, or family sessions. During a therapy session, a person talks with a mental health expert about his or her feelings and problems. Talking through these issues can help the person learn to recognize unhealthy thoughts and behaviors and to replace them with helpful ones. One of the most common types of talk therapy is cognitive-behavioral therapy, in which the patient learns techniques to change negative thoughts and behaviors into positive thinking.

> "Using drugs and alcohol to numb feelings may work in the short term, but substance abuse makes a person feel worse over time.

Research has shown that while mild depressive mood disorders can be treated by talk therapy alone, more severe cases are most effectively treated with a combination of therapy and medication. Antidepressant medications are widely used to treat depression. These medications af-

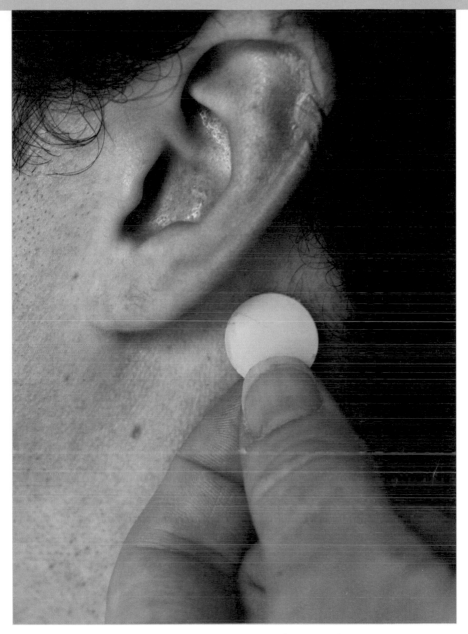

Treatment for severe mood disorders may involve a combination of medication and therapy. One medication being tested for bipolar disorder and depression is administered through a patch placed behind the ear.

fect how brain chemicals called neurotransmitters function and control mood. Several types of antidepressant medications treat depressive disorders, including selective serotonin reuptake inhibitors, tricyclics, and

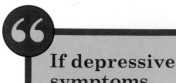

> If depressive symptoms are severe and last for two weeks or more, it may be time to seek help.

monoamine oxidase inhibitors. Bipolar patients may take mood stabilizers like lithium to help even out dramatic mood swings. Experts estimate that 50 percent of unsuccessfully treated mood disorders result from people not taking their medicine properly. Unpleasant side effects, financial costs, and short-term improvement of symptoms all cause people to stop taking mood disorder medication.

Sometimes a patient can be most effectively treated in the hospital. Up to 10 percent of major depressive and 50 percent of manic episodes require hospitalization. This occurs most often when a person displays suicidal or life-threatening behavior. In addition, doctors may consider electroconvulsive therapy, in which short electrical pulses trigger a seizure in the brain for those who are severely depressed, suicidal, or experiencing severe mania.

Lifestyle Changes

Many people with mood disorders have seen improvement in their symptoms and ability to cope with their illness after making certain lifestyle changes. These changes include getting exercise, reducing stress, practicing yoga, getting enough sleep, and eating right. Other people use activities like writing in journals or creating art or music as a healthy outlet for their emotions.

Having a solid support system is another critical part of living successfully with mood disorders. Some find support from family members, friends, or support groups. Nineteen-year-old Kristen finds that talking to family makes her feel better when she is depressed. She says:

> My parents and immediate family have been a huge support to me, especially my Dad because he has experienced so many of the feelings that I do first hand. I know sometimes I get caught up on the fact that our feelings are not caused by the same thing, but they still feel the same regardless and having someone who can truly say they know how it feels really does mean something.[11]

A Hopeful Future

For years mood disorders have been misunderstood. Some people believed the person was just being moody and could snap out of it. Today experts know that a mood disorder is an illness, not a choice. Like other chronic diseases, these disorders need long-term treatment and support. Finding the right treatment may take time, but it can happen eventually. With the right treatment, support, and lifestyle, people with mood disorders can learn to live happy, healthy, and productive lives.

What Are Mood Disorders?

What Are Mood Disorders?

66 **Depression is a prison where you are both the suffering prisoner and the cruel jailor. . . . It is an isolation which changes even your perception of your environment.** 99

—Dorothy Rowe, a woman with major depression.

Mood disorders are a group of mental illnesses that affect the way people think and feel about themselves and the world around them. According to the National Institute for Mental Health, approximately 20.9 million American adults experience a mood disorder each year. Most mood disorders include periods of depression that may vary in intensity. Other typical signs of a mood disorder include decreased interest in activities, loss of self-confidence, and a sense of worthlessness. Severity, duration, and presence of other symptoms separate a mood disorder from normal sadness.

Mood disorders interfere with a person's daily life, affecting sleep, appetite, energy levels, and relationships with others. Family and friends often feel frustrated, guilty, and angry when dealing with a person with a mood disorder. Many wonder why the person cannot just get over the sadness. They may not understand that mood disorders are not a choice. They are illnesses like diabetes, asthma, or heart disease that need long-term treatment and support.

One of the most common mood disorders, major depression, is also known as clinical depression or unipolar depression. Common symptoms include overwhelming sadness, decreased interest in activities, difficulty concentrating, loss of self-confidence, and a sense of worthlessness. Depression can also affect a person's sleep habits, appetite, and energy levels.

Depression affects each person differently. Some people become lethargic, while others appear agitated. Some depressed people sleep all the time, while others experience insomnia. Some people may become incredibly hungry, while others have no interest in food. Many people experience physical and mental symptoms such as fatigue, headaches, stomachaches, and suicidal thoughts. "Depression is not just about being sad about life events. It's a persistent change in what is considered your normal mood," says Laurel Williams, a psychologist at the Adolescent Treatment Program at the Menninger Clinic in Houston. "You're disinterested in life, and you have consistent changes in your sleep and eating habits as well as your energy levels."[12]

Major depression can strike at any age, but it is most commonly diagnosed in people ages 25 to 44. Among adults, women are twice as likely to develop major depression as men. In children major depression occurs at the same rate, regardless of gender. Having a parent or sibling with major depression can increase a person's risk of developing the disorder by 1.5 to 3 times.

Page Hemmis, a carpenter on the television show *Extreme Makeover*, remembered how depression made her feel. She says:

> It's like someone turned the lights off and I was going through the motions in the dark. Give me a broken sink and I can fix it, but I couldn't fix myself. I felt powerless. . . . Nothing gave me pleasure. I would withdraw, because going out and putting on a fake smile was exhausting. . . . I was constantly telling myself to snap out of it. I knew I should be eating better, but I didn't have the strength to make a difference.[13]

Episodes of major depression usually last about 20 weeks. Some people only have a single depressive episode. For other people major depression is a chronic illness. They struggle with repeated depressive episodes separated by periods of normal moods. For some the symptom-free periods may last for years. Others may experience several depressive episodes within a short period of time.

Major depression may be related to certain medical illnesses. Twenty to 25 percent of patients with cancer, diabetes, heart disease, and stroke develop major depression. These people are dealing with the demands of their medical illness and its treatment. They may become less independent or have to make lifestyle changes. The added stress of these challenges makes the person more likely to develop a mood disorder. In addition, a person struggling with major depression is more likely to have other health conditions such as alcohol and drug abuse, anxiety and panic disorders, eating disorders, and obsessive-compulsive disorders.

Dysthymia

Dysthymia is a milder but longer-lasting form of major depression. People suffering from dysthymia may feel gloomy and have difficulty remembering when they last felt happy. They might be inactive and withdraw from others. Others with dysthymia become irritable and have trouble sleeping. To be diagnosed with dysthymia, a patient must experience a continuous depressed mood for at least two years. Women are two to three times more likely than men to be diagnosed with dysthymia.

Because the symptoms of dysthymia are mild and often begin at an early age, many people do not realize that there is anything wrong with their constant depressed feelings. People with dysthymia often wait years before seeking treatment, which makes the illness harder to treat. Early treatment can also help people avoid other mood disorders, social problems, and substance abuse problems.

> **Those who live in higher latitudes, where there are more hours of winter darkness, have a higher risk for SAD.**

Having dysthymia makes a person more likely to develop major depression. About 10 to 25 percent of people with major depression have previously suffered from dysthymia. In some cases a person will develop both disorders at the same time. This condition is called double depression. People with double depression have a greater risk for repeated depressive episodes. They may also have more difficulty recovering from depression.

Seasonal Affective Disorder

When major depression or bipolar disorder occurs in a seasonal pattern, a person may have seasonal affective disorder (SAD). SAD affects a person at specific times or seasons during the year. In most cases depressive symptoms begin during the fall or winter months. During this time SAD sufferers may feel sluggish and have little energy. They might sleep or eat more than usual, particularly carbohydrates that temporarily boost low levels of serotonin. When spring arrives the depression lifts and the person's mood returns to normal.

Women are more likely than men to be affected by SAD. Those who live in higher latitudes, where there are more hours of winter darkness, have a higher risk for SAD. "The shorter, darker days of winter increase the levels of melatonin, a sleep-related hormone, secreted by the pineal gland in the brain. It is thought that the increased level of melatonin is linked to SAD,"[14] says Raymond Crowel, a psychologist and the vice president of mental health and substance abuse services at Mental Health America.

> " People experiencing mania sometimes feel as if they are invincible, which can lead to excessive risk taking. "

Postpartum Depression

In women postpartum depression usually begins within four weeks of giving birth. Although many new mothers experience a short period of sadness after birth called the baby blues, postpartum depression is more severe. Women with this disorder may experience anxiety and panic attacks and may have trouble sleeping. They may cry for no apparent reason and show little interest in their new baby. Some women feel angry toward their baby and may appear agitated. For some the depression is so intense that they have suicidal thoughts.

In some cases of postpartum depression, a woman may experience psychotic features such as delusions or hallucinations. The woman may believe that her baby is evil or magical. Under the grip of these delusions, the woman may try to harm or kill her child. If psychosis is suspected, the woman should immediately receive medical care and possibly be hospitalized. Psychotic symptoms occur in about 1 out of every 500 to 1,000 new mothers.

Postpartum depression affects up to 10 percent of new mothers and is more common after the birth of a first child. Women with postpartum depression are also more likely to experience a recurrence with future births. "This crippling mood disorder has been historically underdiagnosed and undertreated, leaving many mothers at risk, which can lead not only to suicide but possibly to long-term emotional or behavioral problems for the child,"[15] says Sanjay Gupta, chair of the psychiatry department at Olean General Hospital in Olean, New York.

Bipolar Disorder

In bipolar disorder, depression episodes alternate with manic periods. A manic person often becomes euphoric, although some may become angry or irritable. They may talk rapidly and appear distracted or agitated. They may not sleep as much and may have racing thoughts. People experiencing mania sometimes feel as if they are invincible, which can lead to excessive risk taking. Their judgment may seem impaired, and they may engage in reckless or inappropriate behavior. Some people experience delusions and hallucinations.

Actress and author Carrie Fisher was diagnosed with bipolar disorder in her twenties. She says:

> I never shut up. I could be brilliant. I never had to look long for a word, a thought, a connection, a joke, anything. . . . I'd keep people on the phone for eight hours. When my mania is going strong, it's sort of a clear path. You know, I'm flying high up onto the mountain, but it starts going too fast. . . . I stop being able to connect. My sentences don't make sense. I'm not tracking anymore and I can't sleep and I'm not reliable.[16]

There are two types of bipolar disorder, bipolar I and II. People with bipolar disorder I suffer from full-blown manic episodes followed by severe depression periods. Mania can last for days or months, while depression can last for six months or longer.

Bipolar disorder II causes less severe symptoms. The manic phase, hypomania, is less intense than full-blown mania. During hypomania, people may become more outgoing and have more energy and better self-esteem. They may also become more active and productive at work and school. According to Sagar V. Parikh, deputy psychiatrist in chief at the University Health Network in Toronto, the symptoms of bipolar II are subtle, which makes it difficult to see hypomania as part of an illness. "Your highs are mild, your brain is working faster, you have more confidence and energy, you need less sleep—it's the ideal human condition . . . it is difficult to conceptualize it as an illness,"[17] Parikh says. Because their manic phases are less intense, some people with bipolar II are misdiagnosed with depression.

> " The large majority of people with bipolar disorder, 90 percent, will have future cycles of the disorder. "

Bipolar disorder I affects men and women equally, while bipolar II strikes women more frequently. For many people the first manic episode occurs in their teens or twenties. The large majority of people with bipolar disorder, 90 percent, will have future cycles of the disorder.

Each person swings or cycles through bipolar phases differently. Some people cycle between depression and mania over a period of weeks or months. They may experience normal moods between their depression and mania. Others may have more periods of either depression or mania, with occasional bouts of the other. A small number of people, about 10 to 20 percent, may only experience mania. Others have symptoms of depression and mania at the same time, a condition called mixed mania.

Living with Depression

Mood disorders can strike anyone at any time. Philadelphia Eagles offensive lineman Shawn Andrews struggled with depression, anger, and a low self-image for years. After entering the National Football League in 2004, Andrews tried to buy happiness. He surrounded himself with expensive cars and flashy jewelry. Still, none of it made him feel better.

By the summer of 2008, Andrews was miserable. He dreaded getting up in the morning and doubted whether he wanted to continue his football career. All he wanted to do was "sit at home, drown in my sorrows, I guess, and play my music,"[18] he says. When it was time for training camp, Andrews decided he was not going to report, even though he could have been fined $15,000 per week. Instead, Andrews spent his time partying and spending money in an unsuccessful attempt to chase away his melancholy. One day he found himself in his car, speeding at 135 miles per hour (217kph). For a few seconds thoughts of suicide entered his mind. Then his cell phone beeped with a picture message—the smiling face of his 4-month old son. "After that, I just pulled over and cried my eyes out,"[19] says Andrews.

> " Mood disorders are a complicated group of illnesses. The symptoms overlap and appear differently in various people, making these disorders difficult to diagnose correctly. "

Eventually, family members convinced Andrews to seek help. He saw a psychiatrist, who worked with Eagles doctors to coordinate a treatment plan. A year later, in 2009, Andrews had a completely different attitude. "I kind of feel at peace right now vs. where I was last year—just kind of hating everything and everybody. Right now, I'm smiling on the inside and the out,"[20] he says. Andrews knows that he must continue to fight his depression. He follows a treatment program and has assembled a support group of family and friends.

Mood disorders are a complicated group of illnesses. The symptoms overlap and appear differently in various people, making these disorders difficult to diagnose correctly. Still, understanding the types of mood disorders leads to better recognition and treatment.

What Are Mood Disorders?

66 When a person has a depressive disorder, it interferes with daily life, normal functioning, and causes pain for both the person with the disorder and those who care about him or her. 99

—National Institute of Mental Health, "Depression," 2007. www.nimh.nih.gov.

The National Institute of Mental Health is the federal government's chief funding arm for research into mental illnesses.

66 Depression feels like the most isolated place on earth. No wonder they call it a disease of loneliness. 99

—Sally Brampton, *Shoot the Damn Dog: A Memoir of Depression.* New York: Norton, 2008.

Brampton is an author and depression patient.

* Editor's Note: While the definition of a primary source can be narrowly or broadly defined, for the purposes of Compact Research, a primary source consists of: 1) results of original research presented by an organization or researcher; 2) eyewitness accounts of events, personal experience, or work experience; 3) first-person editorials offering pundits' opinions; 4) government officials presenting political plans and/or policies; 5) representatives of organizations presenting testimony or policy.

66 The longer she speaks, the more incoherent she becomes, and the more incoherent she becomes, the more urgent her need is to make us understand her. I feel helpless watching her. 99

—Michael Greenberg, *Hurry Down Sunshine*. New York: Random House, 2009.

Greenberg is an author and the father of a bipolar teen.

66 I've seen the beautiful cartwheel of thoughts pitch past and crash and I've learned not to speak of them, to let them all go. I can stand inside a desperate circus and force my mind to slow, if only for a few moments. It's the hardest work I've ever known. 99

—David Lovelace, *Scattershot: My Bipolar Family*. New York: Dutton, 2008.

Lovelace, an author, is a bipolar patient along with his mother, father, and brother.

66 Bipolar disorder is not easy to spot when it starts. The symptoms may seem like separate problems, not recognized as parts of a larger problem. Some people suffer for years before they are properly diagnosed and treated. 99

—National Institute of Mental Health, "Bipolar Disorder," 2009. www.nimh.nih.gov.

The National Institute of Mental Health is the federal government's chief funding arm for research into mental illnesses.

66 It was like I had big huge weights on my legs and I was trying to swim and just kept sinking. And I'd get a little bit of air, just enough to survive and then I'd go back down again. 99

—Rodolfo, quoted in National Institute of Mental Health, "What Is Depression?" video, February 25, 2010. www.nimh.nih.gov.

Rodolfo is a patient whose struggle with depression is featured in a National Institute of Mental Health video.

66 I have always been depressed, and I have always wanted to fly. . . . Depression, for me, is when you want to be a bird, but can't. **99**

—Caronae Howell, "In Pursuit of Happiness," *New York Times*, July 20, 2009.

Howell is a college student facing depression.

66 Everyone is different, and every depression is different. The common denominator is that depression touches every part of your life. **99**

—Emme and Phillip Aronson, *Morning Has Broken: A Couple's Journey Through Depression*. New York: New American Library, 2006.

Phillip Aronson is a depression patient who has relied on the support of his former wife, supermodel Emme, to deal with his depression.

What Are Mood Disorders?

- About 20.9 million American adults, or **9.5 percent** of the population, have mood disorders, which include major depressive disorder, dysthymia, and bipolar disorder.

- Major depressive disorder is the leading cause of disability among Americans ages **15 to 44**.

- The median age of onset for mood disorders is **30 years**.

- Symptoms of **dysthymia** must persist for at least two years in adults and one year in children to meet criteria for diagnosis.

- Bipolar disorder affects approximately 5.7 million American adults, or about **2.6 percent** of the U.S. population ages 18 and older, in a given year.

- Women experience depression at **twice the rate** of men.

- **Depression** ranks among the top three workplace issues, behind only family crisis and stress.

- Depression's annual toll on U.S. businesses amounts to about **$70 billion** in medical expenditures, lost productivity, and other costs.

Major Depression Is the Most Common Mood Disorder

Mood disorders are a range of illnesses that affect how people think and feel about the world around them. Three of the most common mood disorders are major depression, dysthmia, and bipolar disorder.

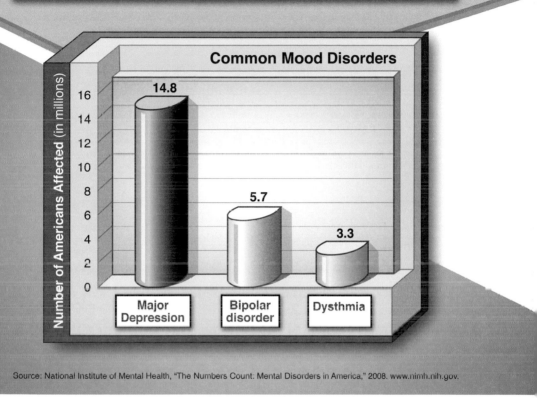

Source: National Institute of Mental Health, "The Numbers Count: Mental Disorders in America," 2008. www.nimh.nih.gov.

- **Sixty to 90 percent** of seasonal affective disorder patients are women.

- More than **two-thirds** of people with bipolar disorder have at least one close relative with the illness or with major depression.

Mental Illness in U.S. Youth Ages 8 to 15

Mood disorders and other mental illnesses can strike children and adolescents. In a survey funded in part by the National Institute of Mental Health and published in 2009, researchers interviewed 3,042 young people and their parents or caregivers to assess the rate of occurrence for five common mental illnesses.

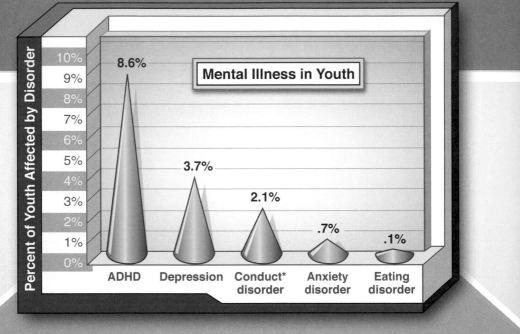

Mental Illness in Youth

Percent of Youth Affected by Disorder

ADHD	Depression	Conduct* disorder	Anxiety disorder	Eating disorder
8.6%	3.7%	2.1%	.7%	.1%

*People with conduct disorder have difficulty following rules and behaving in a socially acceptable manner.

Source: National Institute of Mental Health, "National Survey Tracks Rates of Common Mental Disorders Among American Youth," December 14, 2009. www.nimh.nih.gov.

- Research shows that women with bipolar disorder may have **more depressive episodes** and **more mixed episodes** than men with the illness.

- According to the surgeon general's office, mood disorders are one of the **top 10** causes of worldwide disability.

What Causes Mood Disorders?

"Things are not so simple with depression. We have good ideas about what some of the 'pressures or strains' that result in depression are—but they are not all agreed upon and there might be others."

—The Black Dog Institute, a research facility specializing in mood disorders.

Mood disorders can strike people of any age, gender, race, or social background. The causes of these illnesses are not fully understood, making it impossible to predict who will develop a mood disorder. Most experts believe that there is not one single cause of mood disorders. Instead, they think that mood disorders are caused by a combination of genetic, biological, and environmental factors. "Depression is the convergence of many pathways—genetics, trauma, cognitive patterns and personal setbacks,"[21] says psychologist Rodney Loper.

Having a risk factor, however, does not mean that a person is destined to develop a mood disorder; it only means that his or her statistical chances increase. Many people with risk factors for mood disorders will never develop them. But the more risk factors a person has, the greater chance he or she has of becoming ill. Understanding risk factors can help a person recognize if he or she is vulnerable to mood disorders. With this knowledge, the person can learn about the disorders, warning signs, and treatments.

As children, boys and girls develop depressive mood disorders in equal numbers. When the girls reach adolescence, however, their likelihood of becoming depressed increases. This difference continues into adulthood, when women are twice as likely to develop major depression as men.

The reason women suffer more from depressive mood disorders is unknown. Some believe this occurs because women are more likely than men to be diagnosed and seek treatment. Others suggest that women are more vulnerable because of frequent changes in hormone levels related to monthly menstrual cycles, pregnancy, and menopause. Another possible factor may be the increased stress women face from balancing work and family life.

Unlike depression, bipolar disorder affects men and women equally. Mania is often easier to recognize than depression, which may lead to better identification of this disorder in both genders.

Heredity

Research on mood disorders in families shows that people have a higher chance of developing a disorder if a parent or sibling has a mood disorder. Having a close relative with major depression makes a person 1.5 to 3 times more likely to develop the condition. For bipolar disorder, the family connection is even stronger. According to the National Institute of Mental Health, children with a parent or sibling who has bipolar disorder are 4 to 6 times more likely to develop the illness. Having a close relative with bipolar disorder also increases the chances of a person developing major depression.

> **Most experts believe that there is not one single cause of mood disorders.**

To understand genetic influences on mood disorders, researchers have studied identical twins. They found that when one identical twin develops major depression, the other twin has a 76 percent chance of also developing the illness. Even if the identical twins grow up in different environments, they will both develop the disorder 67 percent of the time. Scientists believe these results indicate a strong genetic component to mood disorders. Because the twins did not both develop a mood disorder in all cases, researchers believe that other factors also play a role in mood disorders.

On the other hand, even if people inherit genes that make them vulnerable to mood disorders, they are not destined to develop these illnesses. "There does seem to be a genetic component to many cases of major depression," says Nurun Shah, an associate professor of psychiatry at the University of Texas at Houston Medical School. "But most people with a family history of depression will not become depressed, and many depression sufferers have no such history."[22]

Because of the family connection, researchers have attempted to identify specific genes that may cause mood disorders. To date, the results of several studies have been inconclusive. Researchers have been unable to identify a single gene linked to mood disorders. Instead, they suspect that several genes

> " Having a close relative with major depression makes a person 1.5 to 3 times more likely to develop the condition. "

may act together to cause a mood disorder vulnerability. While genetic factors may be one cause, researchers still believe that other factors such as environment and brain chemistry influence who develops a mood disorder. "We are still in the early days of understanding how genes and environment interact to increase the risk for depression,"[23] says Thomas R. Insel, director of the National Institute of Mental Health.

Personal History

Having a previous mood disorder can make a person more vulnerable to future episodes. More than half of people with major depression will have a second depressive episode. Most people who have experienced bipolar mania will have future episodes.

Having one mood disorder also increases a person's risk for developing another type of mood disorder. Approximately 10 to 25 percent of people with major depression have also experienced dysthymia. In addition, adolescents with recurring major depression are 10 to 15 percent more likely to develop bipolar disorder.

Brain Structure and Function

The human brain controls basic body functions, movements, thoughts, and emotions. Researchers believe that differences in brain structure and how the brain works may be factors in determining who develops a mood disorder. Brain imaging shows that the brains of people with mood disorders look different than the brains of those without these disorders. In particular, the parts of the brain that regulate mood, thinking, sleep, appetite, and behavior appear to function improperly.

> ❝
> **More than half of people with major depression will have a second depressive episode.**
> ❞

In 2009 a large imaging study at Columbia University Medical Center and the New York State Psychiatric Institute found that people with at least one parent or grandparent diagnosed with depression had a 28 percent thinning of the brain's right cortex compared with study participants with no family history. In addition, the study found that subjects who had additional brain thinning on the left cortex went on to develop depression. Bradley S. Peterson, director of MRI Research in the Department of Psychiatry at Columbia University Medical Center and first author of the study, said:

> Our findings suggest rather strongly that if you have thinning in the right hemisphere of the brain, you may be predisposed to depression and may also have some cognitive and inattention issues. The more thinning you have, the greater the cognitive problems. If you have additional thinning in the same region of the left hemisphere, that seems to tip you over from having a vulnerability to developing symptoms of an overt illness.[24]

Another area of the brain that may influence mood disorders is the limbic system. Within the limbic system, a small structure called the hypothalamus regulates body temperature, sleep, appetite, sexual drive, stress reaction, and other activities. The hypothalamus also works with the adrenal glands to produce adrenaline. If the hypothalamus malfunctions, too much or too little adrenaline may be produced. With too much adrenaline, people may experience mania. With too little adrenaline, they may fall into a depression. In addition, the hypothalamus regulates the pituitary gland, which controls key hormones that may be involved with mood disorders.

Other structures in the limbic system such as the amygdalae and the hippocampus also affect emotions and judgment. Improper functioning of these areas may affect a person's mood and behavior.

Chemical and Hormonal Imbalances

Brain chemistry appears to play a significant role in mood disorders. Chemicals that send signals across gaps between the brain's nerve cells are called neurotransmitters. They affect how a person feels, thinks, and behaves. Research indicates that people with depression and bipolar disorder have neurotransmitter imbalances. These imbalances can cause the messages from the brain to the body to get mixed up or not delivered. When this happens, depressive symptoms may occur.

Two neurotransmitters linked to mood disorders are serotonin and norepinephrine. Some studies suggest that decreased serotonin levels may cause sleep disturbances, irritability, and anxiety. Low levels of norepinephrine have been connected to fatigue and depressed mood.

> **While everyone goes through stressful events, reactions to stress can differ greatly.**

Researchers are also studying how hormones affect mood disorders. Hormones are chemicals that help the body's organs function. For example, the body makes the hormone cortisol in response to stress, fear, or anger. In a typical person cortisol levels peak in the morning, then taper off throughout the day. In people with depression, cortisol levels remain high throughout the day. High levels of cortisol have also been found in people with bipolar disorder. In women, scientists are also studying the effect that cyclical changes in hormones such as estrogen have on brain chemistry and mood disorders. In addition, abnormal thyroid gland function has been linked to bipolar disorder.

Stress Triggers

Life experiences affect a person's thoughts, emotions, and behaviors. Everyone feels sadness and stress when a loved one dies or parents divorce.

Even positive events like a new job or marriage can cause stress. While everyone goes through stressful events, reactions to stress can differ greatly.

> "Growing up with a depressed mother can make a child more vulnerable to depression."

Sometimes, stressful events can trigger a mood disorder, especially if a person is already at risk for developing the disorder.

For some, a single traumatic event is enough to trigger a mood disorder. Situations like death, divorce, or major medical illness create significant emotional turmoil. People can feel as if they have lost control over their lives. For those vulnerable to mood disorders, these events may be enough to trigger depression or bipolar disorder.

When 17-year-old Jeff's parents divorced, he began to experience depression symptoms. He recalls:

> After my dad left, my schoolwork started getting worse. I was sleeping a lot, and I was always in a bad mood. Nothing made me happy, not even baseball, which I love. I had a hard time concentrating. . . .
>
> And then I felt bad physically, too. I'd wake up and I'd feel like I could go to sleep again for another whole day. Sometimes I'd stuff myself with food; other times I could skip meals without even feeling hungry.
>
> . . . I knew something was wrong because I'm not a gloomy kid. But when my parents split up, everything got really bad.[25]

The reasons stress can trigger a mood disorder are unclear. In fact, some people become depressed when there appears to be little stress in their lives. In addition, the same stressful event may trigger depression or bipolar disorder in one person, but not another. For people with chronic depression, repeated depressive episodes may make them more sensitive to stress. When this happens even small stresses can lead to another depression.

Childhood Events

Encountering severe difficulties as a child can make a person more likely to develop a mood disorder. These problems include physical, sexual, or verbal abuse; separation from a parent; an unstable home; or a parent's mental illness. In fact, separation from or the death of a parent before age 11 is the event most significantly linked to mood disorders.

It is not clear why childhood events influence mood disorders in adults. One theory is that children who experience significant difficulties develop low-self esteem and feel powerless to change their lives. These negative feelings may increase a person's vulnerability to mood disorders. Another theory is that early emotional stress can affect the limbic system in a child's developing brain. This could affect his or her ability to regulate emotions as an adult.

In addition, growing up with a depressed mother can make a child more vulnerable to depression. A study at the University of Minnesota in Minneapolis found that having a depressed mother substantially increased a teen's likelihood of becoming depressed, even if he or she was adopted and shared no genetic connection with the mother. When a mother is depressed, it affects her parenting skills and disrupts her child's life, possibly making the child more vulnerable to depression. "There is an environmental liability of maternal depression that cannot be accounted for by genes but that almost certainly interacts with genetic factors to create depression risk in children,"[26] says psychologist and study leader Erin Tully.

Complicated Combination of Factors

Some illnesses have a medical cause that is easy to identify and treat. A person with an ear infection takes antibiotics. People who have diabetes may take insulin to manage their disease. Mood disorders, however, are more complicated. They are not caused by one factor and cannot be simply cured with medication. Instead, mood disorders are a combination of many factors. Although it is difficult to pinpoint the exact cause of mood disorders, understanding risk factors may help a person be more aware of warning signs and make life changes to reduce the risk of developing a mood disorder.

What Causes Mood Disorders?

66 **Bipolar disorder usually lasts a lifetime. Episodes of mania and depression typically come back over time. Between episodes, many people with bipolar disorder are free of symptoms, but some people may have lingering symptoms.** 99

—National Institute of Mental Health, "Bipolar Disorder," 2009. www.nimh.nih.gov.

The National Institute of Mental Health is the federal government's chief funding arm for research into mental illnesses.

66 **Depression is a real and complex illness that is not yet completely understood. We do know that the brains of people with depression are different from those without the illness, but we aren't sure why.** 99

—National Institute of Mental Health, "What Is Depression?" video, February 25, 2010. www.nimh.nih.gov.

The National Institute of Mental Health is the federal government's chief funding arm for research into mental illnesses.

* Editor's Note: While the definition of a primary source can be narrowly or broadly defined, for the purposes of Compact Research, a primary source consists of: 1) results of original research presented by an organization or researcher; 2) eyewitness accounts of events, personal experience, or work experience; 3) first-person editorials offering pundits' opinions; 4) government officials presenting political plans and/or policies; 5) representatives of organizations presenting testimony or policy.

❝Depression is an illness that has a genetic component, and it can recur often, even without obvious stressors.❞

—Sanjay Gupta, in "Women, Weight Gain and Antidepressants," *New York Times*, August 30, 2007. http://health.nytimes.com.

Gupta is the chair of the psychiatry department at Olean General Hospital and a clinical associate professor of psychiatry at the University of Buffalo.

❝No wonder so many of us feel we can't pull ourselves out of the abyss, no matter how hard we try. We have no idea where the descent began.❞

—Mark G. Williams, John D. Teasdale, Zindel V. Segal, John Kabat-Zinn, *The Mindful Way Through Depression: Freeing Yourself from Chronic Unhappiness*. New York: Guilford, 2007.

The authors are internationally renowned cognitive therapy and mindfulness experts.

❝Genetics research indicates that risk for depression results from the influence of multiple genes acting together with environmental or other factors.❞

—National Institute of Mental Health, "Depression," 2007. www.nimh.nih.gov.

The National Institute of Mental Health is the federal government's chief funding arm for research into mental illnesses.

❝In some way, the quiet terror of severe depression never entirely passes once you've experienced it . . . it honors no season and respects no calendar; it arrives precisely when it feels like it.❞

—Daphne Merkin, "A Journey Through Darkness," *New York Times Magazine*, May 6, 2009. www.nytimes.com.

Merkin is a contributing writer for the *New York Times Magazine* and a depression patient.

> **66** If a child is abused in some way—emotionally, physically, or sexually—there is a tremendous loss of self-esteem and this loss can trigger depression. **99**

—Elayne Savage, e-mail to the author, August 1, 2008.

Savage is a psychologist who has treated people with mood disorders for more than 25 years.

> **66** The main cause of bipolar disorder is a chemical imbalance in the brain, but the illness also involves genetic, environmental and other factors. **99**

—Julie A. Fast, "Gold Standard for Treating Bipolar Disorder," HealthyPlace, February 13, 2009. www.healthyplace.com.

Fast is an award-winning mental health author and was diagnosed with bipolar disorder at age 31.

What Causes Mood Disorders?

- Children of depressed parents are **two to three times more** likely to develop depression than children who do not have a family history of the disorder.

- Depression is associated with physical illness. **Twenty-five percent** of hospitalized medical patients have noticeable depressive symptoms, and about **5 percent** are suffering from major depression.

- Depression can be **inherited**. The genetic risk of developing major depression is about **40 percent**, with the remaining **60 percent** being due to environmental factors.

- Each episode of depression increases the risk that the person will experience another episode by **18 percent**.

- **Thirty-three percent** of bipolar patients have at least one bipolar parent.

- Bipolar disorder is frequently inherited. **Genetic factors** are a contributing factor in **80 percent** of cases.

- Some studies suggest that women who experience **postpartum depression** often have had prior depressive episodes.

- It has been found that when one identical twin becomes depressed, the other will also develop clinical depression approximately **76 percent** of the time.

Demographic Risk Factors for Depression

According to the 2009 Gallup-Healthways Well-Being Index, one in six Americans 18 and older reports being diagnosed with depression. Certain demographic groups appear to have a higher risk of depression than others. Groups such as women, divorced or separated people, and those making less than $24,000 annually were more likely to be diagnosed with depression.

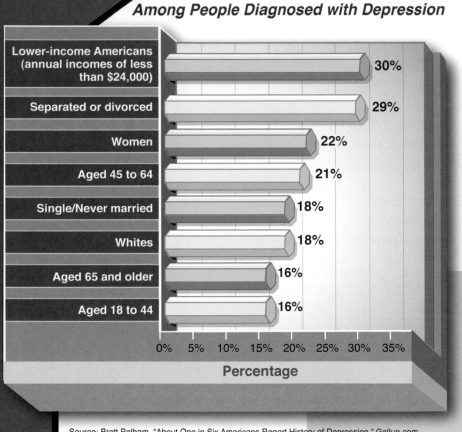

Among People Diagnosed with Depression

Group	Percentage
Lower-income Americans (annual incomes of less than $24,000)	30%
Separated or divorced	29%
Women	22%
Aged 45 to 64	21%
Single/Never married	18%
Whites	18%
Aged 65 and older	16%
Aged 18 to 44	16%

Percentage

Source: Brett Pelham, "About One in Six Americans Report History of Depression," Gallup.com, October 22, 2009. www.gallup.com.

- Episodes of mania and depression are often **linked to the seasons**. Manic episodes are more common during the summer, whereas depressive episodes are more common during the fall, winter, and spring.

Depression Linked to Thinning of Brain Cortex

Researchers have found that people with a family history of depression are likely to have a structural difference in their brains. In these individuals, there is significant thinning of the right cerebral cortex. The cerebral cortex is involved with reasoning, planning, and mood. Thinning in this region may affect the ability to process emotional stimuli, making a person more susceptible to anxiety and depression. This illustration shows a side view of the two hemispheres of the brain. Blue and pink represent thinning, especially pronounced on the right cerebral cortex (right). Areas that are green, most prominent on the left hemisphere, signify little thinning. The patterns seen here are consistent with a person who has a family history of depression.

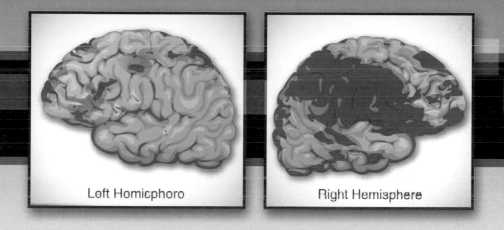

Left Hemisphere | Right Hemisphere

Source: Roni Caryn Rabin, "Study Links Depression to Thinning of Brain's Cortex," *New York Times*, March 24, 2009.

- When one parent has bipolar disorder, the risk of developing the disorder to each child is **15 to 30 percent**. When both parents have bipolar disorder, the risk increases to **50 to 75 percent**.

- Some **20 percent** of adolescents with major depression develop bipolar disorder within five years of the onset of depression.

- For children the most significant traumatic event linked to depression is **separation from or death of a parent** before the age of 11.

How Do Mood Disorders Affect People?

66Most kids who are depressed will function poorly in at least one of these three domains—at home, at school, or with friends—and many will function poorly in all of them.99

—Maureen Empfield, director of psychiatry at Northern Westchester Hospital Center in Mount Kisco, New York, and coauthor of *Understanding Teenage Depression*.

Mood disorders can be devastating to those affected, as well as to their families and friends. These disorders can affect a person's life in many ways. They impair a person's ability to sleep, eat, and work. They damage relationships with family and friends. Mood disorders can also cause a person to feel bad about him- or herself, lowering self-esteem and confidence. In addition, people with mood disorders are more likely to engage in risky behavior.

Diagnosed at age 14, Maleah from Syracuse, New York, remembers how it felt to live with depression. She writes:

> I felt emotionally disconnected from everyone at school, and I was (and still am) always tired. My friends didn't like to hang out with me because they were confused as to why I was acting this way (spacey), or thought I was boring. I quit my instrument, and found the easiest of

tasks ridiculously stressful. It felt like there was a thick plastic coating all over me, blocking me from saying what I was screaming inside. Since I couldn't release that voice, it came out in crying.[27]

Physical Effects

Mood disorders are not just a psychological illness—they also affect people physically. For people with mood disorders, changes in appetite, sleep patterns, and energy levels are common. How the disorder affects each person varies. Some people may lose interest in food. Others find themselves more hungry than usual. Some people find that they are tired all the time and sleep more than usual. Others develop insomnia and spend hours awake. Courtney, a teen diagnosed with major depression, says that she was "permanently tired, regardless of how much sleep I got. Some days it was too much effort even to get out of bed."[28]

Mood disorders can also cause headaches, stomachaches, back pain, and other chronic aches and pains. In fact, one European study found that people with depressive or anxiety disorders are at least twice as likely to wake up with a headache as those who do not have the disorders. For Sherri Walton, depression led to chronic stomach problems and frequent bouts of bronchitis. "I'd feel terrible for no reason and just withdraw,"[29] she says.

> " People with mood disorders often report that they have problems functioning and thinking normally while they are depressed. "

Generally, as a mood disorder's severity increases, so do the number and intensity of physical symptoms. Because they do not feel well, many people find that continuing daily activities becomes a tremendous struggle.

Emotional Impact

People with mood disorders frequently feel like their emotions are out of control. They may feel intensely happy or extremely sad. Jenn, who lives near Boston, Massachusetts, remembers how depression affected her emotions as a teen. "I would cry at the drop of a hat and take whatever they [family and friends] said personally. Sometimes I would cry for no reason and wouldn't know why,"[30] she says. Other people find their anger erupts at the smallest annoyance.

Mood disorders can also make people feel emotionally distant. "I always felt outside the mainstream," says 33-year-old Saritza Velilla, diagnosed with major depression. "I could feel alone in a roomful of people. . . . I did not develop emotionally and had trouble relating to others."[31]

Cognitive Effect

Mood disorders can disrupt a person's cognitive abilities. People with mood disorders often report that they have problems functioning and thinking normally while they are depressed. Some people find they have trouble remembering details and are easily distracted. Others find that they have difficulty making a decision and sticking with it.

Cognitive problems can interfere with a person's performance at work and school. People in intellectually demanding jobs such as professors or doctors may suddenly find themselves unable to focus. For children and teens, cognitive problems may affect their grades at school. Kristen was diagnosed with depression at age 13 and remembers how she struggled at school. "My concentration when I'm depressed flatlines. I can remember sitting at school and having teachers talk to the class . . . and just feel like nothing is going in and nothing made sense. I knew I wasn't stupid, I was just frustrated and then the more frustrated I got the more emotional I got and it all went downhill from there,"[32] she says.

Many depressed people also report that they have negative thoughts about themselves and their lives. Some researchers believe that this occurs because the depressed mind's impaired cognitive skills limit a person's ability to feel hope.

Losing Hope and Feeling Worthless

People with a pattern of negative thinking are more likely to develop major depression. Often they have negative thoughts about themselves, the world and people around them, and the future. Depressed people frequently dwell on past mistakes and failures. They blame themselves for things that are not their fault and are out of their control. For example, if a teen gets a bad grade because his depression makes it difficult to concentrate, he may take the failure as proof that he is a bad person. Battered by negative thoughts, depressed people's self-esteem and confidence drop and they feel helpless to control their own life and happiness. Soon they lose hope that the future will improve.

A depressed person can quickly become overwhelmed by negative thoughts. "I kept thinking about how horrible I felt, how I hated my life, how I hated me, how easy it would be to put an end to all my suffering. I loved the life Emme and I had built together, but I hated what it had become, what I had become,"[33] wrote Phillip Aronson, former husband of supermodel Emme, about his struggle with depression.

Risky Behavior

For some people mood disorders lead to poor decisions and risky behaviors. Many depressed people feel like they cannot cope with their feelings of depression. To escape they might turn to risky behaviors. Getting into fights, using drugs and alcohol, having promiscuous sex, and self-cutting are all signs a person may be in a serious depression. "If you're depressed you're more likely to abuse substances, and take risks you wouldn't otherwise,"[34] says Margaret Grey, dean of the Yale University School of Nursing.

Cassandra first experienced major depression in the seventh grade. To relieve her pain, she started cutting. "The first time I self-injured, *I thought this is gonna be trouble.* I never used drugs or alcohol, but I continued cutting throughout seventh grade and kept it a secret from everyone,"[35] she says. Before long, Cassandra's arms and legs were covered in small slashes that she tried to hide from family and friends. "I thought cutting was helping me, but it wasn't. . . . It was making everything ten times worse. I had to hide from everyone and lead a double-life,"[36] she remembers.

> " **Men in particular may appear aggressive and exhibit risky behavior to cope with a mood disorder.** "

Men in particular may appear aggressive and exhibit risky behavior to cope with a mood disorder. "He might blow off paying bills, spend excessively, and crave sex constantly or even start abusing booze and drugs,"[37] says Yvonne Thomas, a Los Angeles psychologist.

For bipolar sufferers, most risky behavior occurs during a manic phase. During mania, the person feels elated and optimistic. He or she is on top of the world and feeling invincible. While riding the manic high, a bipolar person may go on a wild spending spree, take physical risks, or have impulsive sexual relationships with strangers. Nineteen-year-old Zack described how mania led him to risky behavior: "I felt invincible, like I was on top of the world and could do anything. I even thought I had psychic powers, like ESP. I didn't sleep because I felt like it was a waste of time. . . . I spent a thousand dollars on CDs, clothes, and food for my friends."[38]

Effect on Relationships

Mood disorders often cause people to act differently around family, friends, and coworkers. They may cry easily or become quickly irritated. While depressed, people may withdraw from family and friends. Activities that once interested them no longer hold any appeal. Erratic behavior and mood swings can cause problems in relationships with other people.

Mood disorders can also cause problems at work and school. In the middle of a depressive period, a person may miss days of work or school because he or she cannot get out of bed. When at work or school, performance may suffer because that person cannot concentrate and is easily distracted. Rob had just received his GED and started a new job when depression struck. His sadness turned into anger, and he lashed out at family and friends. When his brother suggested that he see a doctor, Rob refused at first. "But after a few weeks, I started having problems at work too," Rob recalls. "Sometimes I wouldn't show up because I wasn't able to sleep the night before. When I got fired, I knew I had to listen to my brother and get help."[39]

> "Close family members and friends are often intensely affected by a loved one's mood disorder."

Close family members and friends are often intensely affected by a loved one's mood disorder. Emme Aronson, a full-figured supermodel, seemed to have the perfect life, with a successful career, a loving husband, and a new baby daughter. Soon after the birth of their daughter, however, Emme's husband, Phillip, started his descent into major depression. According to Emme, Phillip's depression had a devastating effect on her. She says:

> Each day, it seemed we'd lose another piece of Phil. . . . There was no end to it, and I remember thinking that no one else could see what I see. No one knows what it was like, to be caught up in it like we were. We had an amazing group of supportive friends, and our families couldn't have been more caring, but it's a lonely thing to be married to a man in the depths of a depression with an infant daughter at home. . . . It was all about getting through each day. I'd never felt more alone.[40]

Suicide

It is not uncommon for people to think about ending their life while they are depressed. According to the American Foundation for Suicide Prevention, at least 90 percent of people who kill themselves have a psychiatric illness such as major depression, bipolar disorder, or another depressive illness. In addition, a person's risk of suicide increases if his or her mood disorder is untreated. In fact, untreated depression is the number one risk for suicide among youth. Suicide is the third leading cause of death in 15- to 24-year-olds and the fourth leading cause of death in 10- to 14-year-olds.

In addition to mood disorders, other factors contribute to a person's risk of suicide. People who have attempted suicide in the past are 20 to 50 percent more likely to kill themselves than someone who has not attempted suicide. People with a family history of suicide or an impulsive personality are more likely to take their own life. Males are three times more likely to commit suicide than females. Biological factors may also increase suicide risk. Researchers have found a connection between low levels of a serotonin metabolite called 5-HIAA in the cerebrospinal fluid and increased suicide rates.

> " **Untreated depression is the number one risk for suicide among youth.** "

From a young age, Kurt Cobain, the lead singer of the rock band Nirvana, struggled with untreated bipolar disorder. At the height of his fame in April 1994, Cobain shot himself at home. He was the third member of his family to commit suicide. Cobain's suicide note revealed some of the pain he was hiding inside. "I haven't felt the excitement of listening to as well as creating music along with reading and writing for too many years now. I feel guilty beyond words about these things. . . . The worse crime I can think of would be to rip people off by faking it and pretending as if I'm having 100 percent fun,"[41] he wrote.

> Despite having to deal with the physical, emotional, cognitive, and social effects of mood disorders, many people are able to live normal and productive lives.

While his death shocked fans, Cobain's cousin Beverly Cobain, a registered nurse with mental health experience, may have been less surprised. "His risk was very high: untreated bipolar disorder, drug addiction, prior suicides of family members, alcohol, violence and unpredictability in his childhood, poor self-esteem, violence in his married life. Kurt could have been a poster child for risk of suicide,"[42] she says.

Coping with Mood Disorders

Despite having to deal with the physical, emotional, cognitive, and social effects of mood disorders, many people are able to live normal and productive lives. In fact, some very successful people have been diagnosed and treated for mood disorders, including sports stars, actors, writers, and politicians. The list includes Counting Crows singer Adam Duritz, actress Brooke Shields, astronaut Buzz Aldrin, best-selling author Amy Tan, and former football player Terry Bradshaw. These people and many others show it is possible to cope with a mood disorder and live a successful, productive life.

How Do Mood Disorders Affect People?

❝I couldn't sit down for a minute really to do anything that took deep concentration.❞

> —Rodolfo, quoted in National Institute of Mental Health, "What Is Depression?" video, February 25, 2010.
> www.nimh.nih.gov.

Rodolfo is a patient whose struggle with depression is featured in a National Institute of Mental Health video.

....

❝I was worn down, and desperate for some kind of help. . . . I had been strong for Phil, for the longest time, and it had gotten us nowhere . . . there was no relief, and no end in sight.❞

> —Emme and Phillip Aronson, *Morning Has Broken: A Couple's Journey Through Depression*. New York: New American Library, 2006.

Emme is a world-famous model who supported her former husband, Phillip, during his battle with major depression.

....

* Editor's Note: While the definition of a primary source can be narrowly or broadly defined, for the purposes of Compact Research, a primary source consists of: 1) results of original research presented by an organization or researcher; 2) eyewitness accounts of events, personal experience, or work experience; 3) first-person editorials offering pundits' opinions; 4) government officials presenting political plans and/or policies; 5) representatives of organizations presenting testimony or policy.

Primary Source Quotes

"One of my scary behaviors was to take my car out . . . and get it cranking, and then close my eyes. . . . It was a like a giant game of chicken, and the stakes were life and death, and I was playing to lose."

—Emme and Phillip Aronson, *Morning Has Broken: A Couple's Journey Through Depression.* New York: New American Library, 2006.

Phillip Aronson is a depression patient who relied on the support of his former wife, supermodel Emme, to deal with his depression.

....

"When I did speak, it was mostly about my wish to commit suicide, a wish that was never all that far from my mind but at times like these became insistent."

—Daphne Merkin, "A Journey Through Darkness," *New York Times Magazine*, May 6, 2009. www.nytimes.com.

Merkin is a contributing writer for the *New York Times Magazine* and a depression patient.

....

"It's very much an uphill battle to diagnose and intervene to prevent suicide in a free society where patients have choices and, because of depression, hopelessness and discouragement, may have given up on the possibilities for recovery."

—Jan A. Fawcett, quoted in Medscape Psychiatry and Mental Health, "Assessing Suicide Risk in Patients with Bipolar Disorder: An Expert Interview with Jan A. Fawcett," January 22, 2008. www.medscape.com.

Fawcett is a professor of psychiatry at the University of New Mexico School of Medicine in Albuquerque and has devoted his career to the study of mood disorders and suicide.

....

"When I am depressed it makes all my relationships feel tense. I feel like I don't care about anyone or anything, including myself."

—Kristen, e-mail to the author, July 18, 2008.

Kristen is a college student diagnosed with depression and generalized anxiety disorder with panic attacks.

....

66 People with bipolar disorder are often seen as out-of-control, lazy, difficult or just plain crazy. This makes sense when looking from the outside, as a person with constantly changing moods can be very hard to live with.**99**

—Julie A. Fast, "Gold Standard for Treating Bipolar Disorder," HealthyPlace, February 13, 2009. www.healthyplace.com.

Fast is an award-winning mental health author and was diagnosed with bipolar disorder at age 31.

66 I had a horrible time sleeping. . . . I would put it off for hours because I knew that once I laid down I would never get to sleep anyway.**99**

—Melissa, e-mail to the author, July 18, 2008.

Melissa was diagnosed with depression as a teenager.

How Do Mood Disorders Affect People?

- Four times as many men as women die by **suicide**, although women attempt suicide two to three times as often as men.

- More than **90 percent** of people who kill themselves have a diagnosable mental disorder, most commonly a depressive disorder or a substance abuse disorder.

- Depressive disorders often **co-occur** with anxiety disorders and substance abuse.

- **Thirty percent** of teens with depression also have a substance abuse problem.

- People with depression are four times as likely to have a **heart attack** as those without a history of the illness.

- **Fifty percent** of people with **Parkinson's disease** may experience depression.

- **Untreated depression** is the number one risk for suicide among youth.

- U.S. workers with bipolar disorder averaged **65.5 lost workdays** in a year, compared to 27.2 for those with major depression.

Physical Effects of Mood Disorders

For most people, mood disorders are more than a psychological illness, they also cause uncomfortable and sometimes dangerous physical symptoms.

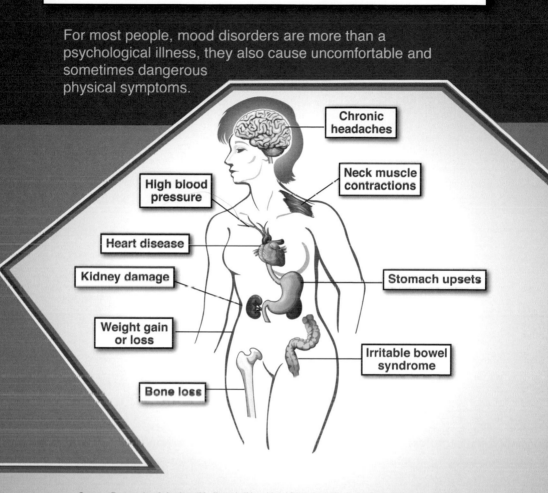

Chronic headaches

Neck muscle contractions

High blood pressure

Heart disease

Kidney damage

Stomach upsets

Weight gain or loss

Irritable bowel syndrome

Bone loss

Source: Depression & Anxiety (Medletter), "How Mood Disorders Affect Your Body," January 2009, p. 3.

- One in four people with **cancer** also suffers from major depression.

- In one study **52 percent** of severely depressed people reported that they lost their sense of humor.

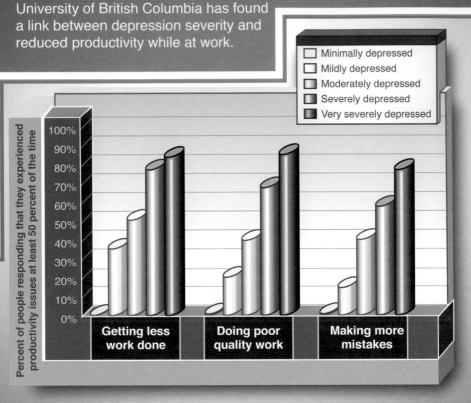

Depression at Work

Mood disorders, especially depressive disorders, can significantly affect a person's performance at work. Many studies have found that major depression is linked to more absences or time away from work. In addition, a 2009 study from researchers at the University of British Columbia has found a link between depression severity and reduced productivity while at work.

Legend:
- Minimally depressed
- Mildly depressed
- Moderately depressed
- Severely depressed
- Very severely depressed

Y-axis: Percent of people responding that they experienced productivity issues at least 50 percent of the time

Categories: Getting less work done | Doing poor quality work | Making more mistakes

Source: BMC Psychiatry, "A New Clinical Rating Scale for Work Absence and Productivity: Validation in Patients with Major Depressive Disorder," December 3, 2009. www.ncbi.nlm.nih.gov.

- Low self-esteem is reported by **81 percent** of severely depressed people.

- **Seventy-six percent** of severely depressed people reported difficulty in making decisions.

Depression Increases the Likelihood of Trying Drugs and Alcohol

A national study, released in 2007, found links between depression and first-time use of drugs and alcohol among young people. According to the National Survey on Drug Use and Health, depressed young people were more likely to take their first drink of alcohol or try illegal drugs than their peers who do not have depression.

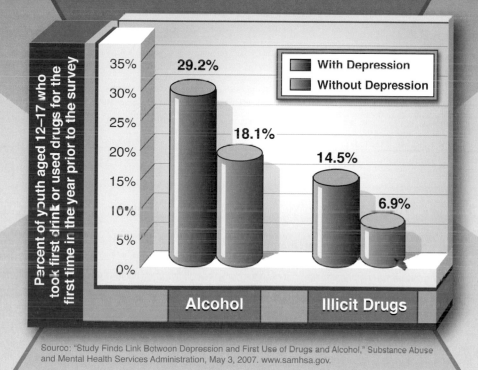

Source: "Study Finds Link Between Depression and First Use of Drugs and Alcohol," Substance Abuse and Mental Health Services Administration, May 3, 2007. www.samhsa.gov.

What Treatments Are Available for Mood Disorders?

❝There are lots and lots of reasons why we should prevent and treat early depression and all of the terrible functional and psychosocial consequences that depression brings. We need to create greater public awareness of those consequences and the availability of treatments, and to develop more robustly effective treatments.❞

—Adolescent brain expert Bradley S. Peterson of New York-Presbyterian Morgan Stanley Children's Hospital.

Like other illnesses, mood disorders can be treated. Up to 80 percent of patients treated see an improvement in symptoms within four to six weeks. Early diagnosis and treatment, however, are very important. The earlier treatment begins, the more effective it can be in preventing a recurrence of symptoms. Left untreated, mood disorders can become serious and linger for months or even years.

Getting a Diagnosis

The first step in recovering from a mood disorder is getting an accurate diagnosis. Because most mood disorders have similar depressive symptoms, they are hard to distinguish from each other and from other illnesses. Diagnosing bipolar disorder in particular can be tricky. The mood swings of bipolar disorder may be mistakenly diagnosed as major depression, ADHD, or borderline personality disorder. For some, it may take years before their bipolar disorder is correctly diagnosed and treated.

If no physical cause for depressive symptoms is found, the doctor or a trained mental health professional may conduct a psychiatric interview. During the interview, he or she will ask questions about the patient's symptoms and family or personal history of mood disorders. The mental health professional will also ask about life at home, school, and work, if the patient is using drugs or alcohol, and if the person has had any suicidal thoughts. If the

> " Up to 80 percent of patients treated see an improvement in symptoms within four to six weeks. "

mental health professional diagnoses the person with a mood disorder, he or she will develop a treatment plan. Some people with milder symptoms do well with talk therapy alone. Patients with more severe depression may respond better to a combination of talk therapy and medication. Bipolar patients may need a combination of several medications.

Talk Therapy

Talk therapy or psychotherapy is a common mood disorder treatment. Talk therapy can consist of individual, group, or family sessions. During a session the patient talks to an expert about his or her feelings and problems and learns ways to deal with them. "Finding a therapist who believes in recovery is the first step," says Saritza Velilla, a 33-year-old diagnosed with major depression. "Someone who can teach you to think differently and learn new behaviors. . . . My therapist finally put a name to what I'd been feeling since I was 7 years old."[43]

The most common types of talk therapy are cognitive-behavioral therapy (CBT) and interpersonal therapy. CBT is based on the idea that people's thoughts influence their feelings and behaviors. Negative thoughts about a situation will lead to negative feelings and behaviors. Therefore, the goal of CBT is to change how people think about a situation and to teach them ways to respond more positively and feel better. A 2009 study in the *Journal of the American Medical Association* reported that CBT works well for adolescents with depression. After six months teens assigned to CBT sessions were less likely to become depressed than teens assigned to traditional talk therapy. Mary Alvord, a psychologist in Maryland, uses CBT to help children and teens change negative behaviors. "All good therapies have similarities—forging a relationship, trust. But with CBT, you work with what the person wants to change in a very direct manner. You're collaborating in a more direct way than with traditional therapy,"[44] she says.

Interpersonal therapy focuses on a patient's relationships with others. The therapist helps the patient understand how interacting with other people affects his or her moods. During interpersonal therapy the patient learns strategies to develop healthier relationships with family and friends.

Medications

For moderate to severe depression and bipolar disorder, a person may need medication to manage his or her illness. Antidepressant medications work by adjusting mood-related brain chemicals such as serotonin and norepinephrine to normal levels. There are several types of antidepressants, including selective serotonin reuptake inhibitors, tricyclics, and monoamine oxidase inhibitors. A doctor may prescribe several antidepressants or adjust dosages until he or she finds the best medication or combination of medications for a patient. "Clinicians tell us that different drugs seem to work for different people," says Thomas Laughren, team leader for the review of psychiatric drugs in the U.S. Food and Drug Administration's Division of Neuropharmacological Drug Products. "And it's difficult to predict which people will respond to which drug or who will experience what side effects."[45]

> Because mood disorders affect each person differently, each patient's treatment plan will also be different.

For bipolar patients, mood stabilizers help smooth out mood swings. The most commonly prescribed mood stabilizer is lithium. It works by controlling the amount of the neurotransmitter glutamate in the brain. Glutamate levels that are too high can trigger a manic episode, whereas levels that are too low can cause a depressive episode. In addition to lithium, patients with bipolar disorder often take other medications. A doctor may prescribe antidepressants, anti-anxiety medication, or antipsychotic medication.

Some patients decide to stop taking medication without their doctor's approval. Some stop because they feel better, whereas others do not like the side effects, which can include nausea, insomnia, and weight gain. Because most medications take up to eight weeks to be fully effective, some patients stop because they think the medicine is not working. Patients who stop their medication too soon risk a return of their mood disorder.

> " Patients who stop their medication too soon risk a return of their mood disorder. "

Pete Earley's son has bipolar disorder. When his son stops taking his medication, Earley says his son's behavior becomes bizarre and irrational. "Part of my son's illness is believing he is perfectly fine when he goes off his medicines," says Earley. "You are asking an irrational person to make a rational decision. It's like expecting a person with a broken leg to run a marathon."[46]

Other Treatments

In addition to talk therapy and medication, other treatments are available for mood disorders. Five to 10 percent of major depression episodes and up to 50 percent of manic episodes require hospitalization. This occurs when symptoms are severe and the person displays life-threatening behavior. In the hospital, doctors and nurses closely monitor patients and can provide intense therapy.

For severe cases that do not respond well to medication and talk therapy, electroconvulsive therapy (ECT) may be used. ECT is especially effective for those who are extremely depressed, suicidal, or experiencing severe mania. During ECT, electrodes deliver electrical impulses to locations on the head. Although the patient does not feel the impulses, the electrical stimulation causes a 30-second seizure in the brain. Doctors believe ECT affects the chemical balance of the brain's neurotransmitters. "It is the most effective and rapidly acting treatment for severe depression,"[47] says Sarah Lisanby, a professor of clinical psychiatry at Columbia University Medical Center.

After unsuccessfully battling depression and bipolar disorder for years with therapy and medication, a University of Kansas student sought out ECT. She says that after a few sessions, "I literally went from almost unable to function—feeling suicidal—to a 180-degree change."[48]

> " Some people use art and writing as a way to release stress. "

ECT is not without risks. Short-term memory loss is one of the most common side effects. While memory may return after treatment ends, some problems may remain. The Kansas student, for example, now uses a daily planner and makes lists to help her memory, things she did not do before ECT.

For people with seasonal affective disorder (SAD), light therapy is an effective treatment. Patients spend about a half hour per day in front of a specially designed light box that mimics outdoor light. Doctors believe that the intense light causes a biochemical change in the brain that lifts mood and reduces SAD symptoms.

Lifestyle Changes

While it is not always possible to prevent mood disorders, certain lifestyle changes can reduce the risk of developing symptoms. Eating well, exercising, and getting enough sleep are all good ways to keep the body in balance. Exercise also releases chemicals called endorphins into the brain, a natural way to lift mood and boost energy.

Managing stress is another way to reduce vulnerability to mood disorders. Some people use art and writing as a way to release stress. Other stress busters include simplifying and cutting back on unnecessary activities, staying positive, and learning to recognize warning signs. "If your depression comes from stress—working sixty-hour weeks with no recreation—you have to address that issue first,"[49] says psychologist and author Richard O'Connor.

Another key to managing mood disorders is getting support. "Isolating yourself is not good. Get out among people or in nature, so you're not alone with your own mind,"[50] recommends O'Connor. Support may come from family, friends, a good therapist, or a support group of people who have experienced mood disorders. Sometimes just being around other people can help reduce symptoms. Many people find that joining a support group and meeting others with the same or similar experiences helps them manage their disorder. Lifestyle changes are not a cure for mood disorders, but they can reduce factors that contribute to them.

Emerging Treatments

Several emerging treatments may soon be an option for patients when standard depression treatments do not work. Transcranial magnetic stimulation (TMS) is currently being studied as a potential treatment for patients with major depression. During TMS a special electromagnet placed on the patient's scalp generates short magnetic pulses. The pulses pass through the skull and stimulate the brain. Research has shown that TMS can alter brain chemistry and relieve depression. It can be as effective as antidepressants in relieving depression symptoms, without the side effects of medication. To date, TMS has not been approved by the Food and Drug Administration and is only available through research studies.

Another new treatment is vagus nerve stimulation (VNS). The vagus nerve is a main communication link between the body's major organs and the brain. VNS therapy uses a small pulse generator implanted in the chest and connected to the vagus nerve. The generator sends small pulses to the vagus nerve, which in turn delivers the pulses to the brain. VNS therapy targets the areas of the brain that control mood and depression symptoms. VNS therapy has been approved by the Food and Drug Administration for people 18 years old and older who have chronic treatment-resistant depression.

> " One of the greatest barriers to treatment is the stigma of having a mental illness. "

One of the newest treatments being studied is magnetic stimulation therapy. This type of therapy uses a magnetic field to induce a seizure, similar to electroconvulsive therapy. Researchers hope to concentrate magnetic stimulation therapy on specific areas of the brain affected by mood disorders.

When Treatment Does Not Work

For some people mood disorder treatment does not ease symptoms or prevent recurrences. An estimated 50 percent of the unsuccessful depression treatments failed because of people not taking their medicine or taking it incorrectly. Those who take medicine as prescribed but still report symptoms may suffer from treatment-resistant depression or bipolar disorder. In these cases doctors may try multiple medications and combinations of therapy to try to relieve a patient's symptoms.

Despite treatment success rates, some people do not seek treatment for their mood disorders. In fact, the National Institute for Mental Health reported that only about half of Americans diagnosed with major depression in a given year receive treatment. In addition, only one-fifth receive treatment that is consistent with current guidelines.

Nontreatment and undertreatment of mood disorders stem from many factors, including lack of health insurance, financial barriers, and lack of education about treatment benefits. In addition, one of the greatest barriers to treatment is the stigma of having a mental illness. Many people may be afraid to tell others about their symptoms and ask for help. Men, in particular, think that having a mental illness is a sign of weakness and are less likely to seek treatment.

Living Successfully with Mood Disorders

Many mood disorder patients successfully manage their symptoms with a combination of medication, talk therapy, and lifestyle changes. They surround themselves with a strong support system that can help during difficult times and educate themselves about their disorder. In addition, emerging new treatments like transcranial magnetic stimulation, vagus nerve stimulation, and magnetic stimulation therapy bring hope for treating mood disorders in the future.

When dealing with mood disorders, perseverance counts. Because these disorders affect each person differently, it may take time to find the right combination of treatments to ease symptoms. Tracy's story shows how sticking it out through depression treatment can lead to success. "I started taking medicine and was in counseling, but after four months, I still didn't feel a lot better. But I continued to work with my doctors, and as a team, we found a medicine that helped me. Gradually, I began to feel better. It was a long process, but with help, I was able to get through it."[51]

66 While we can't alter our genetic predisposition, positive steps can be taken to minimize or prevent further depression episodes. . . . These can include improving your self-awareness, resolving emotional conflicts, exercising regularly and avoiding alcohol. 99

—Sanjay Gupta in "Women, Weight Gain and Antidepressants," *New York Times*, August 30, 2007.
http://health.nytimes.com.

Gupta is the chair of the psychiatry department at Olean General Hospital and a clinical associate professor of psychiatry at the University of Buffalo.

66 One of the most hurtful statements was when a friend asked me, 'Do you WANT to get better?' which suggests that getting better is only a matter of willing ourselves to get better. 99

—Therese Borchard, in "Surviving Depression: An Interview with Therese Borchard," Psych Central, January 15, 2010.
http://blogs.psychcentral.com.

Borchard is the author of *Beyond Blue: Surviving Depression and Anxiety and Making the Most of Bad Genes* and is a depression patient.

* Editor's Note: While the definition of a primary source can be narrowly or broadly defined, for the purposes of Compact Research, a primary source consists of: 1) results of original research presented by an organization or researcher; 2) eyewitness accounts of events, personal experience, or work experience; 3) first-person editorials offering pundits' opinions; 4) government officials presenting political plans and/or policies; 5) representatives of organizations presenting testimony or policy.

66Will I ever 'get over' my treatment resistant depression? Will I ever be free of medications? Probably not. But the amount may decrease with time as I begin to fill in the holes of the floor beneath me—and carefully watch my step.99

—Julie, "Sleeping In and Seeping Out: A Look at Treatment Resistant Depression," Depression and Bipolar Support Alliance, March 27, 2006. www.dbsalliance.org.

Julie is a depression patient.

66I firmly believe we have made a great start in understanding mental illnesses and that in our lifetimes we will be able to treat and even prevent mental illnesses with much greater certainty and speed.99

—Statement of Thomas Insel, House Committee on Energy and Commerce, Subcommittee on Health, June 28, 2006.

Insel is the director of the National Institute of Mental Health.

66Even now, I am still recovering, and I keep trying to push myself gently towards where I want to go in life and friends I like to spend time with. This has been hard, but recovery is a slow process.99

—Jessie James, "A Story About Recovery," Depression and Bipolar Support Alliance, November 20, 2008. www.dbsalliance.org.

James is a bipolar patient who was diagnosed at age 17.

66Medication helped me get stable enough to deal with my emotions and talk about my feelings.99

—Kara, telephone interview with the author, August 14, 2008.

Kara is a teen who has struggled with severe depression.

66 My very first evaluation was overwhelming because you're hearing all of this terminology that sounds absolutely terrible. . . . Nothing is wrong with *you* personally, it's an imbalance, and I had to reiterate that to myself a lot. 99

—Jenna, e-mail to the author, September 8, 2008.

Jenna was diagnosed at age 12 with depression and an anxiety disorder.

66 Medication is half the battle, but stress management and living a healthy lifestyle are also key to health maintenance. 99

—Eliza Richmond, in "The Many Faces and Facets of BP," *BP*, Summer 2007. www.bphope.com.

Richmond is a 28-year-old from Maine with bipolar disorder.

What Treatments Are Available for Mood Disorders?

- Only about **50 percent** of Americans diagnosed with major depression in a given year receive treatment for it.

- A depressive episode, left untreated, can last six months, or **chronically for years**.

- **Ten million** people in the United States are taking prescription antidepressants.

- Depression is one of the most treatable illnesses: **80 to 90 percent** of patients find relief with treatment.

- A common medication, lithium, is effective in controlling mania in **60 percent** of individuals with bipolar disorder.

- An estimated **50 percent** of unsuccessful treatment for depression is due to **medical noncompliance**.

- Support group participants are **86 percent** more willing to take medication and cope with side effects.

- Up to **10 percent** of major depressive and **50 percent** of manic episodes require hospitalization.

Response to Electroconvulsive Therapy

In a 2009 study funded by the National Institute of Mental Health, electroconvulsive therapy was equally effective for patients with depression and patients with bipolar disorder. Most of the study patients had not responded to previous treatment with multiple medications. During the trial, the participants received electro-convulsive therapy three times per week for at least 10 weeks.

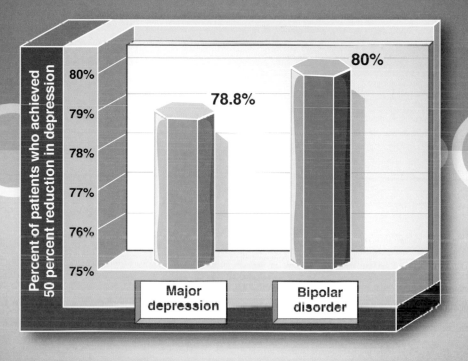

Source. *Psychiatric Times*, "Patients with Bipolar and Unipolar Depression Show Similar Response to Electroconvulsive Therapy," December 14, 2009. www.psychiatrictimes.com.

- It may take up to **10 years** for people with bipolar disorder to receive an accurate diagnosis, with only 1 in 4 receiving an accurate diagnosis in less than 3 years.

- Women are far more likely to be misdiagnosed with **depression**, and men are far more likely to be misdiagnosed with **schizophrenia**.

Race and Ethnicity Affect Likelihood of Receiving Depression Treatment

In 2009, scientists from Wayne State University, the University of Michigan, the University of California in Los Angeles, and the Harvard School of Public Health reported results on mood disorder care by ethnic and racial groups. The study found that while the rate and severity of major depression was similar between the groups studied, the level of care differed and appeared to be linked to access to mental health care.

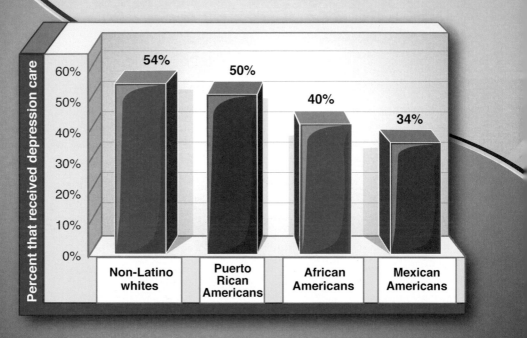

Source: National Institute of Mental Health, "Just Over Half of Americans Diagnosed with Major Depression Receive Care," January 4, 2010. www.nimh.nih.gov.

- **Cognitive behavioral therapy** is not a traditional, long-term talk therapy. Instead, it usually lasts no more than 20 sessions.

- **Eighty to 90 percent** of people who live with a serious mental illness are unemployed.

Combination Therapy for Treatment-Resistant Depression

In a study published in the February 27, 2008, *Journal of the American Medical Association*, researchers found that teens treated with a combination of talk therapy and medication for depression fared better than those treated with medication alone. The teens in the study had previously been treated unsuccessfully for depression with a two-month course of antidepressants. Because about 40 percent of adolescents with depression do not respond well to their first try with antidepressant medication, the study findings may help physicians and therapists make more effective treatment choices.

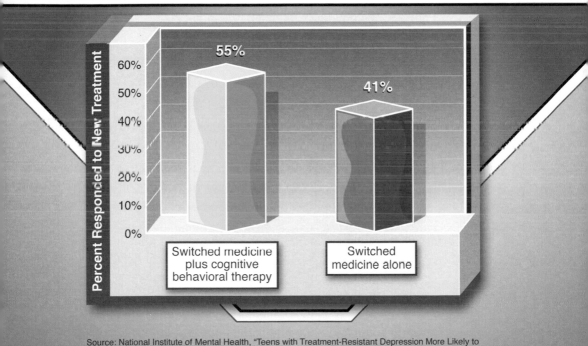

Source: National Institute of Mental Health, "Teens with Treatment-Resistant Depression More Likely to Get Better with Switch to Combination Therapy," February 26, 2008. www.nimh.nih.gov.

Key People and Advocacy Groups

American Psychiatric Association: Publisher of the *Diagnostic and Statistical Manual of Mental Disorders*, the American Psychiatric Association guides the country's 38,000 psychiatrists on how to treat mental illnesses, including mood disorders. The association's advocacy efforts include educating the public about mental health, psychiatry, and successful treatment options.

Terry Cheney: Cheney is a bipolar patient who has written a memoir about her struggle with bipolar disorder. She is an attorney and the daughter of former vice president Dick Cheney.

Winston Churchill: The prime minister led Great Britain during World War II while struggling with bipolar disorder.

Depression and Bipolar Support Alliance: The alliance is the leading patient-directed national organization focusing on depression and bipolar disorder. It works to ensure that people living with mood disorders are treated equitably. It also supports research to promote more timely diagnosis, develop more effective treatments, and discover a cure.

Carrie Fisher: Best known as Princess Leia in the *Star Wars* trilogy, the actress was diagnosed with bipolar disorder at age 24. In her book *Postcards from the Edge*, Fisher wrote about rehabilitation, ECT, and her recovery from her illness and drug addictions.

Mental Health America: The organization is the country's largest and oldest community-based network, with more than 300 affiliates dedicated to helping all people live mentally healthier lives. The organization advocates for policy change, educates the public, and provides community programs and services.

National Alliance on Mental Illness (NAMI): The NAMI is a grass-roots mental health advocacy organization that works to increase awareness, provide education, and advocate for policy change that improves the lives of people with mental illnesses, including mood disorders.

National Institute of Mental Health (NIMH): The NIMH is one of the world's leading mental health organizations. It conducts and supports research on the causes, diagnosis, prevention, and treatment of depression and other mood disorders.

Jane Pauley: Pauley is a bipolar patient who has authored a memoir in recent years recounting her struggle with bipolar disorder. Pauley is a well-known TV journalist.

Brooke Shields: A well-known actress who wrote about her experience with postpartum depression in her book *Down Came the Rain*, Shields has also spoken out about removing the social stigma of postpartum depression.

William Styron: Pulitzer Prize–winning novelist Styron wrote *Darkness Visible: A Memoir of Madness*, a detailed account of his struggles with depression, in 1990.

Mike Wallace: An editor of the top-rated *60 Minutes* television news program, Wallace developed depression during a long court trial in which his integrity and judgment were questioned daily. Years after seeking treatment, Wallace spoke out on television about his experience with depression, hoping to inspire people to seek help.

Chronology

400 B.C.

Hippocrates-trained physicians believe melancholia is caused by an excess of black bile in the body. Purging and removal of blood are treatments.

1952

The American Psychiatric Association publishes the first *Diagnostic and Statistical Manual of Mental Disorders* (*DSM*), which is still used today by clinicians and researchers in the United States and around the world to diagnose mental disorders, including mood disorders.

A.D. 1800s

During the nineteenth century *depression* emerges as a term for a mental disorder characterized by a reduced emotional state.

1937

Italian researchers Ugo Cerletti and Lucio Bini introduce electrically induced seizures to treat mental illness, the only form of electroconvulsive therapy accepted today.

B.C.   1800   1900   1930   1955

1917

Austrian psychoanalyst Sigmund Freud likens the state of melancholia to mourning in his paper "Mourning and Melancholia." Freud also emphasizes that early life experiences are a predisposing factor.

1946

President Harry Truman signs the National Mental Health Act, calling for a National Institute of Mental Health to conduct research into mind, brain, and behavior and thereby reduce mental illness. The National Institute of Mental Health is formally established on April 15, 1949.

1924

American psychologist Mary Cover Jones introduces a behavioral therapy approach to help children unlearn fears. Behavioral therapy would eventually be merged with cognitive therapy to form cognitive behavioral therapy.

1949

Australian researcher John Cade reports the benefits of lithium in treating 10 patients with mania.

1957
Iproniazid, one of the first antidepressants, is synthesized. It was originally developed as a treatment for tuberculosis but became widely prescribed in the late 1950s to treat depression.

2010
Advanced brain imaging techniques give scientists an opportunity to study and identify specific circuits that are involved in mood disorders and study the effectiveness of medical and behavioral treatments.

1985
The Chicago, Illinois–based Depression and Bipolar Support Alliance is founded, becoming one of the largest national organizations to provide support to people with mood disorders.

2005
Actress Brooke Shields releases her book, *Down Came the Rain*, about her struggle with postpartum depression.

1970
Lithium is approved by the U.S. Food and Drug Administration to treat mania.

1955

1985

2010

1966
Psychiatrists Jules Angst of Switzerland and Carlo Perris of Sweden conclude that depression and bipolar disorder are separate mood disorders.

1980
The American Psychiatric Association officially changes the name of manic depression to bipolar disorder.

1994
After struggling with untreated bipolar disorder for years, rock superstar Kurt Cobain commits suicide. His death brings awareness of the risks of untreated mood disorders to many across the United States.

1975
The National Institute of Mental Health Conference on Depression in Childhood officially recognizes depression in children.

1979
The National Alliance for the Mentally Ill (NAMI) is founded to provide support, education, advocacy, and research services for people with serious psychiatric illnesses.

Related Organizations

American Academy of Child and Adolescent Psychiatry

3615 Wisconsin Ave. NW

Washington, DC 20016

phone: (202) 966-7300 • fax: (202) 966-2891

Web site: www.aacap.org

The academy is a national professional medical association dedicated to treating and improving the quality of life of children, adolescents, and families affected by mental, behavioral, or developmental disorders.

American Foundation for Suicide Prevention (AFSP)

120 Wall St., 22nd Floor

New York, NY 10005

phone: (888) 333-2377 • fax: (212) 363-6237

e-mail: inquiry@afsp.org • Web site: www.afsp.org

The AFSP is the leading national not-for-profit organization dedicated to understanding and preventing suicide through research, education, and advocacy and to reaching out to people with mental disorders and those affected by suicide. The foundation funds scientific research, offers educational programs about mood disorders and suicide prevention, promotes legislation relating to suicide prevention, and provides resources for people at risk and people whose loved ones have committed suicide.

American Psychiatric Association

1000 Wilson Blvd., Suite 1825

Arlington, VA 22209

phone: (888) 357-7924

e-mail: apa@psych.org • Web site: www.psych.org

The American Psychiatric Association has over 38,000 U.S. and international member physicians working together to ensure humane care and effective treatment for all persons with mental disorders. It publishes many books and journals, including the widely read *American Journal of Psychiatry.*

American Psychological Association

750 First St. NE

Washington, DC 20002-4242

phone: (800) 374-2721

e-mail: public.affairs@apa.org • Web site: www.apa.org

The American Psychological Association represents more than 148,000 American psychologists, who study and treat human behavior. The association's Web site features information about psychology topics, including mood disorders, and contains links to many publications.

Association for Behavioral and Cognitive Therapies

305 Seventh Ave., 16th Floor

New York, NY 10001

phone: (212) 647-1890 • fax: (212) 647-1865

Web site: www.abct.org

This association represents therapists who provide cognitive behavioral therapy for people who suffer from many types of mental illnesses, including mood disorders. The association's Web site features fact sheets on mental illnesses, including depression and bipolar disorders.

Child and Adolescent Bipolar Foundation

820 Davis St., Suite 520

Evanston, IL 60201

phone: (847) 492-8519

e-mail: cabf@bpkids.org • Web site: www.bpkids.org

The Child and Adolescent Bipolar Foundation is a parent-led, not-for-profit, Web-based membership organization of families raising children diagnosed with, or at risk for, pediatric bipolar disorder. Visitors to the foundation's Web site can find information about bipolar disorder, current research, and listings of doctors who treat bipolar disorder.

Depression and Bipolar Support Alliance

730 N. Franklin St., Suite 501

Chicago, IL 60654-7225

phone: (800) 826-3632 • fax: (312) 642-7243

e-mail: info@dbsalliance.org • Web site: www.dbsalliance.org

The Depression and Bipolar Support Alliance has more than 400 community-based chapters that provide support for people with mood disorders and their families. The alliance provides educational materials to schools, the media, and other interested groups. It also lobbies in Washington, D.C., for laws that support mental health education and research.

Families for Depression Awareness

395 Totten Pond Rd.

Waltham, MA 02451

phone: (781) 890-0220

Web site: www.familyaware.org

Families for Depression Awareness is a nonprofit organization that helps sufferers and their families recognize and cope with depression and bipolar disorders. The group's Web site features information about mood disorders and symptoms, support groups, and family profiles.

Mental Health America

2000 N. Beauregard St., 6th Floor

Alexandria, VA 22311

phone: (800) 969-6642 • fax: (703) 684-5968

Web site: www.nmha.org

Mental Health America is an advocacy group for people with mental illnesses and their families. The group's Web site features many resources, including fact sheets on mood disorders, information on finding support groups, and information on how to take action to support research and funding for mental illnesses.

National Alliance on Mental Illness (NAMI)

Colonial Place Three

2107 Wilson Blvd., Suite 300

Arlington, VA 22201-3042

phone: (703) 524-7600 • fax: (703) 524-9094

Web site: www.nami.org

The NAMI is an advocacy group for people with mental illnesses and includes local chapters in every state. The alliance offers education programs and services for individuals, family members, health care providers, and the public. The NAMI also serves as a voice for Americans with mental illness, working in Washington, D.C., and state houses across the country.

National Institute of Mental Health (NIMH)

6001 Executive Blvd.

Bethesda, MD 20892-9663

phone: (866) 615-6464

e-mail: nimhinfo@nih.gov • Web site: www.nimh.nih.gov

The NIMH is the federal government's chief funding agency for mental health research in America. The institute's Web site provides fact sheets and information about mental illness, including mood disorders, and the latest science news and research on these illnesses.

For Further Research

Books

Emme and Phillip Aronson, *Morning Has Broken: A Couple's Journey Through Depression*. New York: New American Library, 2006.

Terri Cheney, *Manic: A Memoir*. New York: William Morrow, 2008.

Beverly Cobain, *When Nothing Matters Anymore: A Survival Guide for Depressed Teens*. Minneapolis, MN: Free Spirit, 2007.

Russ Federman and J. Anderson Thomson, *Facing Bipolar: The Young Adult's Guide to Dealing with Bipolar Disorder*. Oakland, CA: New Harbinger, 2010.

Leslie Garis, *House of Happy Endings: A Memoir*. New York: Farrar, Straus and Giroux, 2007.

S. Nassir Ghaemi, *Mood Disorders: A Practical Guide*. Philadelphia: Lippincott Williams & Wilkins, 2008.

Michael Greenberg, *Hurry Down Sunshine*. New York: Other Press, 2008.

Marya Hornbacher, *Madness: A Bipolar Life*. Boston: Houghton Mifflin, 2008.

Periodicals

Nicholas Bakalar, "Long-Term Therapy Effective in Bipolar Depression," *New York Times*, April 10, 2007.

Paul Chi and Liza Hamm, "My Depression Nightmare," *People*, September 21, 2009.

Andy Coghlan, "Young and Moody or Mentally Ill?" *New Scientist*, May 19, 2007.

Dennis Dillon, "No More Darkness," *Sporting News*, August 3, 2009.

Sarah Wassner Flynn, "Coming Out of the Darkness," *Girls' Life*, December 2008/January 2009.

Mark Grimsley, "What If . . . Churchill Hadn't Tamed His 'Black Dog'?" *World War II*, May 2009.

Caronae Howell, "In Pursuit of Happiness," *New York Times*, July 20, 2009.

Donna Jackel, "Accepting the Diagnosis," *BP*, Summer 2009.

Jen Kovacs, "Beyond the Baby Blues," *Esperanza*, Spring 2009.

Daphne Merkin, "A Journey Through Darkness," *New York Times Magazine*, May 6, 2009.

Michelle Roberts, "The Mask of Male Depression," *Esperanza*, Spring 2009.

Michelle Tan and Kathy Ehrich Dowd, "Skating Through Sadness," *People*, October 8, 2007.

Nancy Tobin, "The Wit and Wisdom of Carrie Fisher," *BP*, Winter 2010.

Alex Tresniowski and Michaele Ballard, "Madness and Forgiveness," *People*, March 31, 2008.

Liz Welch, "Getting Her Life Back," *Real Simple*, October 2007.

Internet Sources

American Psychiatric Association, "Bipolar Disorder," 2010. www.healthy minds.org/Main-Topic/Bipolar-Disorder.aspx.

Black Dog Institute, "Depression Explained," 2010. www.blackdoginsti tute.org.au/public/depression/depressionexplained/index.cfm.

Mayo Clinic, "Depression (Major Depression)," 2010. www.mayoclinic. com/health/depression/DS00175.

National Alliance on Mental Illness, "Bipolar Disorder," October 2006. www.nami.org/Template.cfm?Section=By_Illness&Template=/ TaggedPage/TaggedPageDisplay.cfm&TPLID=54&ContentID =23037.

National Institute of Mental Health, "What Is Depression?" video, February 25, 2010. www.nimh.nih.gov/health/topics/depression/index. shtml.

Source Notes

Overview

1. Quoted in Families for Depression Awareness, "Terrie, Age 54, with Major Depression." www.familyaware.org.
2. Quoted in Families for Depression Awareness, "Terrie, Age 54, with Major Depression."
3. Quoted in Maureen Empfield and Nicholas Bakalar, *Understanding Teenage Depression*. New York: Henry Holt, 2001, p. 17.
4. Quoted in Families for Depression Awareness, "Missy, Bill, and Katherine." www.familyaware.org.
5. Quoted in David Gutierrez, "Psych Setback: New Study Demolishes Genetic Link to Depression," Natural News, November 4, 2009. www.natural news.com.
6. Quoted in All About Depression, "What Is Depression?" September 9, 2004. www.allaboutdepression.com.
7. Quoted in All About Depression, "What Is Depression?"
8. Quoted in National Institute of Mental Health, "Mood Disorders Predict Later Substance Abuse Problems," January 9, 2008. www.nimh.nih.gov.
9. Darren, "Real Student Stories—Darren," Students Against Depression. www.studentdepression.org.
10. Quoted in Sarah Wassner Flynn, "Coming Out of the Darkness," *Girls' Life*, December 2008/January 2009.
11. Kristen, e-mail interview with the author, September 10, 2008.

What Are Mood Disorders?

12. Quoted in Flynn, "Coming Out of the Darkness."
13. Quoted in Paul Chi and Liza Hamm, "My Depression Nightmare," *People*, September 21, 2009.
14. Raymond Crowel, "From the Expert: Quotes on Seasonal Affective Disorder (SAD)," Mental Health America, 2010. www.mentalhealthamerica.net.
15. Quoted in Gerlad Secor Couzens, "Women, Weight Gain and Antidepressants," *New York Times*, August 30, 2007. http://health.nytimes.com.
16. Quoted in David Staba, "Hollywood Kid Carrie Fisher and Her Best Awful," *BP*, Fall 2004. www.bphope.com.
17. Quoted in *BP*, "Accepting the Diagnosis," Summer 2009. www.bphope.com.
18. Quoted in Dennis Dillon, "No More Darkness," *Sporting News*, August 3, 2009, pp. 28–31.
19. Quoted in Dillon, "No More Darkness," pp. 28–31.
20. Quoted in Dillon, "No More Darkness," pp. 28–31.

What Causes Mood Disorders?

21. Quoted in HealthyPlace, "Living with Clinical Depression: The 'Common Cold' of Mental Health," March 2, 2009. www.healthyplace.com.
22. Quoted in National Institute of Mental Health, "Much Touted 'Depression Risk Gene' May Not Add to Risk After All," June 16, 2009. www.nimh.nih.gov.
23. Quoted in Annie Murphy Paul, "Heredity and Depression," *Shape*, April 2003, p. 44.
24. Quoted in Live Science, "Depression Linked to Brain Thinning," March 26, 2009. www.livescience.com.
25. Quoted in Empfield and Bakalar, *Understanding Teenage Depression*, pp. 113–14.

26. Quoted in Bruce Bower, "Mom Can Increase Her Child's Risk of Depression via Nurture Alone: New Study Suggests Fathers Don't Have the Same Influence," *Science News*, October 11, 2008, p. 9.

How Do Mood Disorders Affect People?

27. Maleah, e-mail interview with the author, July 19, 2008.
28. Quoted in Empfield and Bakalar, *Understanding Teenage Depression*, p. 33.
29. Quoted in Liz Welch, "Getting Her Life Back," *Real Simple*, October 2007.
30. Jenn, e-mail interview with the author, August 14, 2008.
31. Quoted in Carol Lewis, "The Lowdown on Depression," *FDA Consumer*, January/February 2003, p. 28.
32. Kristen, e-mail interview with the author, July 18, 2008.
33. Emme and Phillip Aronson, *Morning Has Broken: A Couple's Journey Through Depression*. New York: New American Library, 2006, p. 116.
34. Quoted in Julie Mettenberg, "Risky Business," *Countdown*, Spring 2006, p. 11.
35. Quoted in Families for Depression Awareness, "Cassandra: Age 19, Major Depression, with Mother." www.familyaware.org.
36. Quoted in Families for Depression Awareness, "Cassandra."
37. Quoted in Theresa O'Rourke, "When Guys Get the Blues," *Cosmopolitan*, November 2007, p. 40.
38. Quoted in Families for Depression Awareness, "Zack and Nancy." www.familyaware.org.
39. Quoted in All About Depression, "How Depression Affects a Person's Life," September 9, 2004. www.allaboutdepression.com.
40. Emme and Aronson, *Morning Has Broken*, pp. 107–108.
41. Quoted in Bipolar Lives, "Kurt Cobain Suicide Note," 2009. www.bipolar-lives.com.
42. Beverly Cobain, "Even in His Youth," A Healthy Me, April 28, 2009. www.ahealthyme.com.

What Treatments Are Available for Mood Disorders?

43. Quoted in Lewis, "The Lowdown on Depression," p. 28.
44. Quoted in Nancy Shute, "Prevent Depression in Teens with Cognitive Behavioral Therapy," *U.S. News & World Report*, June 4, 2009. www.usnews.com.
45. Quoted in Lewis, "The Lowdown on Depression," p. 28.
46. Quoted in Lewis, "The Lowdown on Depression," p. 28.
47. Quoted in Sarah Baldauf, "If the Gloom Won't Lift," *U.S. News & World Report*, December 2009. www.usnews.com.
48. Quoted in Baldauf, "If the Gloom Won't Lift."
49. Quoted in D.G., "How Depression Differs," *Town & Country*, August 2009.
50. Quoted in D.G., "How Depression Differs."
51. Quoted in Mental Health America, "Factsheet: Dealing with Treatment-Resistant Depression: What to Do When Treatment Doesn't Seem to Work," 2010. www.mentalhealthamerica.net.

List of Illustrations

List of Illustrations

Index

adrenaline, 38
Aldrin, Buzz, 54
Alvord, Mary, 64
American Foundation for Suicide Prevention, 53
Andrews, Shawn, 27–28
antidepressants, 18–20, 64
Aronson, Phillip, 31, 55, 56

bipolar disorder, 11, 26–27, 30, 44
    development of recurring major depression and, 37
    diagnosis of, 62–63
        length of time in making, 73
    genetic factors and, 45
    percent of affected people with close relative having, 33
    prevalence of, 32, 33 (chart)
    response rate for electroconvulsive therapy, 73 (chart)
    risky behavior/substance abuse in, 15–17
Black Dog Institute, 35
Borchard, Therese, 69
Bradshaw, Terry, 54
brain
    cerebral cortex, effects of depression on, 47 (illustration)
    chemical/hormonal imbalances in, 13, 39, 64–65
    electroconvulsive therapy and, 65
    electromagnetic stimulation of, 67

structure and function, 37–39
Brampton, Sally, 29

Centers for Disease Control and Prevention (CDC)
children/adolescents
    abuse and depression in, 44
    bipolar disorder in, 47
    cognitive-behavioral therapy for, 63–64
    gender differences in depression in, 11
    with mothers having depression, risk for major depression among, 41
    occurrence of mental illness in, by type, 34 (chart)
Cobain, Beverly, 54
Cobain, Kurt, 54
cognitive-behavioral therapy, 63–64, 74
cortisol, 13, 39
Crowel, Raymond, 25

delusions, in postpartum depression, 25
depression. See major depression
disability
    major depressive disorder as leading cause of, 32
    mood disorders and, 34
Duritz, Adam, 54
dysthymia, 11, 24
    depression and, 37
    prevalence of, 33 (chart)
    symptoms of, 32

Picture Credits

Cover: iStockphoto.com
Maury Aaseng: 33–34, 46–47, 59–61, 73–75
AP Images: 19
Photos.com: 16

About the Author

Carla Mooney is the author of many books for young adults and children. She lives in Pittsburgh, Pennsylvania, with her husband and three children.